Mindful Master:

10 Minutes a Day to Less Stress, Less Worry, More Peace, and More Resilience

by Nick Trenton

www.NickTrenton.com

Table of Contents

CHAPTER 1. THE ART OF BEING PRESENT — 7

A HISTORICAL PERSPECTIVE: FROM THE EAST TO THE WEST, AND FROM RELIGION TO SCIENCE — 20
MINDFULNESS IN PLAIN ENGLISH — 33

CHAPTER 2. EVERYDAY MINDFULNESS FOR MENTAL CALM — 45

READING, WRITING, AND LISTENING MINDFULLY — 56

CHAPTER 3. MELDING MINDFULNESS WITH MEDITATION — 77

MEDITATION FOR NOVICES AND VETERANS — 77
A MINDFUL FRAMEWORK — 86
CHALLENGES AND OBSTACLES WITH MENTAL CHATTER — 91

CHAPTER 4. HOW TO OVERCOME AND DEFEAT EVERYDAY ERUPTIONS — 111

FOR THE BUSY BEE — 112
FOR THE PERPETUALLY DISSATISFIED — 118

CHAPTER 5. A PATH TO FULFILMENT AND SATISFACTION — 135

GAINING AWARENESS TO BREAK BAD HABITS AND ENHANCE SELF-CONTROL — 136
HOW TO EASE EMOTIONAL TURMOIL — 147
MINDFULNESS: KINDNESS, AND COMPASSION, AND EMOTIONAL INTELLIGENCE — 154

SUMMARY — 175

Chapter 1. The Art of Being Present

"Meditation is not evasion; it is a serene encounter with reality."
- *Thích Nhất Hạnh*

Today the word "mindfulness" is seemingly everywhere. People now speak of mindfulness and meditation not only in the realm of temples and retreats, but also in the workplace, schools, hospitals, government, the military and even the sports field. Researchers have studied the effect mindfulness has on our productivity, resilience, and well-being, and now neuroscientists are even investigating the effect meditation has on our brains.

But most of us would be hard-pressed to come up with a concise definition of mindfulness if put on the spot. What does it *really mean*?

Is it some wishy-washy Buddhist concept that promises peace of mind, ecstasy, and enlightenment? Is it a stress management technique?

Both?

If you think that mindfulness is more or less the same as meditation, you're partly right, although there's a little more to it. In 2012, the American Psychological Association gave their definition of mindfulness as "a moment-to-moment awareness of one's experience without judgment. In this sense, mindfulness is a state and not a trait. While it might be promoted by certain practices or activities, such as meditation, it is not equivalent to or synonymous with them."

Mindfulness is essentially awareness—but it's a *certain quality of awareness* that we can cultivate within ourselves.

While it's so easy these days to rush in with our personal opinions, appraisals, and judgments of every stimulus, mindful awareness is characterized by a complete nonattachment to the sensations and thoughts we become aware of. Instead of reacting to every transient thought or feeling that arises within us, being mindful is like taking a step back to *watch ourselves* having that emotion, or that thought.

In **becoming aware of our thoughts as thoughts**, we gain some distance from them, and give ourselves the opportunity to choose to become engaged—or not.

Now, while that could be taken to mean that mindfulness leads us to disengage from the present reality, this could not be further from the truth. The key to awareness is that it is always based in the present.

Awareness and mindfulness are not theories or fixed personality traits, but something we do and *experience*, continually, moment after moment. While anxious rumination can take us away from the immediate moment in front of us and either back to the remembered past or into the imagined future, mindfulness is about being fully present with what's going on right here, right now. And what are we meant to be aware of? Thoughts, physical sensations, emotions, or a blend of all three.

Mindfulness can be a concept too abstract and elusive to grasp without effort, but understanding it becomes a little easier when we consider what happens when we're not engaged in it.

When we are not mindful, we are simply not paying attention. We see but we don't really look; we hear but we don't really listen. Without mindfulness, we go through our lives like robots on autopilot. If you've ever eaten a meal without actually tasting it, found yourself at home with no memory of having driven yourself there, or zoned out in a conversation with a friend, you know what it means to not be in control of your own conscious awareness. When we are distracted, unconscious, or acting mindlessly, we are not in our full awareness—and this includes any time we get carried away with worries for the future or regrets about the past.

We lack mindfulness when we act without noticing what we're really doing. Without mindfulness, we are unable to fully focus or concentrate, departing from the present and getting carried away by our thoughts. We act without thinking, getting pulled this way and that by our shifting experiences, as though we're walking through life half-asleep.

Many people have claimed that mindfulness is accompanied by an attitude of compassion, while others would describe this perspective more as a kind of acceptance—an acknowledgement of the moment and yourself within it, however you are. No judgment or interpretation. No clinging or rejecting.

Combining the above facets and features, we can thus boil all of this down to a workable, clear definition of what mindfulness is: *a state of non-judgmental awareness of the present moment, which we can access through certain practices, such as meditation.*

The Benefits of a Mindfulness Practice

What can mindfulness help with?

The answer is: everything.

This may seem like a grandiose claim, but it's only because when we talk about mindfulness, we are talking about the very lived quality of our experience in each passing moment, no matter what we are doing, thinking or feeling. In this way, mindfulness doesn't specialize—it's a skill that can be applied any time we are able to pause and become aware of the moment we are having, as we are having it (i.e. always!).

People have been touting the benefits of daily meditation for years, but there is now considerable scientific evidence for the many benefits associated with increased mindfulness in general. Though there are some empirical challenges with measuring a fleeting state of mind, research is accumulating to show that mindfulness does indeed promote emotional self-regulation, stress reduction, and mental well-being.

Research done in 2006 by Walsh and Shapiro into mindfulness practices such as tai chi and yoga has shown that these techniques can train heightened awareness and greater concentration and focus. The goal with many such disciplines is to master voluntary control over conscious awareness itself, so that such awareness can be directed at will. When you are able to control and direct your own awareness, you are better able to allot attention and beam targeted focus on your present experience.

Mindfulness also results in an increased sense of calm along with what is called *metacognition*—the ability to think about your own thinking. Have you ever seen those movie scenes wherein the soul leaves the body, then watches everything that happens to and around the (now unconscious) body? In a way, metacognition works something like that. The main differences are that in metacognition, you don't need your soul to depart from your body, nor does the rest of you become unconscious. In metacognition, you only need to recognize that a part of your mind can somehow "detach" from the rest of you and then watch and think about the thoughts that occur in your mind. When re able to wield this ability at will, the benefits can be innumerable. As you watch your own thoughts, you can avoid being consumed and enslaved by them, especially by those automatic thoughts that only serve to wreck your calm and inner peace. Through metacognition, you gain power over your thoughts, and not the other way around.

Another benefit of mindfulness is the strengthened ability to unplug from rumination and switch off anxious thinking. When you're stressed out and overwhelmed by the events unfolding in front of you, it's easy to succumb to your mind's narrative of what could go wrong and how powerless you are to stop the cascade of unfortunate events that will soon commence. When you practice mindfulness, you learn to curb such narratives and realize you have the power to choose how you respond in every situation. The result? An enhanced sense of well-being.

What does "well-being" mean in this context? Typically, it refers to a general state of good mental health that encompasses a range of aspects: lower stress and reactivity along with better cognition, focus, memory, as well as mental flexibility, and even more satisfying relationships.

In 2008, Chambers and colleagues asked twenty amateur meditators to attend a ten-day mindfulness retreat, then compared their responses on a self-report inventory with those of a control group who didn't meditate. The group that meditated claimed to have higher mindfulness levels, and also improved mood and fewer symptoms of depression, anxiety, and rumination (i.e. anxious overthinking). Surprisingly, they also demonstrated the ability to sustain attention on a task at a much higher level than their non-meditating peers.

A meta-study by Hoffman et. al. done in 2010 analyzed thirty-nine other mindfulness studies and concluded that mindfulness-based stress reduction (MBSR) or mindfulness-focused cognitive therapy could have significant therapeutic benefits for the treatment of mood disorders and a range of psychological issues. Stress reduction is one of these benefits.

Norman Farb and six of his colleagues found in 2010 that some of these effects could even be seen in the brain—by using an fMRI, they found that those who meditated showed less neural reactivity when watching a sad film compared to those who didn't meditate. In many mindfulness practices, people essentially learn better emotional regulation, exerting a level of control and selectivity over the feelings they experience, so much so that their actual neural function is altered.

Another study also conducted in 2010 by Jha and colleagues compared a military group who had attended a mindfulness course for eight weeks with control groups of civilians who didn't meditate, as well as military who didn't meditate. The working memory capacity of the nonmeditating military was the worst, and the meditating military group the best—in other words, the more a person meditated, the higher the chance they would self-report better mood and demonstrate enhanced working memory.

This might not surprise you if you're a meditator yourself. Those who meditate teach themselves to tune out distracting sensations and information if they choose to, and sustain attention on a single focus for longer. This translates to greater cognitive flexibility, i.e. the ability to take control of and direct one's attention at will.

Mindfulness doesn't just give you greater conscious mastery over your own thoughts, but over your feelings too. "Reactivity" describes the spontaneous, knee-jerk emotional reaction we may have to inner or outer stimuli—a rude comment from someone, a scary movie, or an upsetting memory you recall at three o'clock in the morning.

A 2007 study by Ortner and colleagues showed two groups of people some upsetting pictures. Those who routinely meditated were far more able to disengage emotionally than those who didn't. This disengagement could come down to the ability to self-observe—to step outside of emotions and thoughts rather than getting tangled and identified with them.

Self-awareness essentially disengages you from the automatic neural pathways associated with certain emotional responses. By being mindful, we give ourselves the chance to learn to respond to emotional stimuli in a new way. Or not respond at all! This is a superpower, when you think about it—the ability to adapt your brain's response to stressful or difficult situations so you can achieve more equanimity and mental resilience.

Gaëlle Desbordes, a professor of radiology at Harvard Medical School and a neuroscientist at the Martinos Center for Biomedical Imaging, found encouraging neuroscientific evidence to suggest that mindfulness-based therapies can help those with depression. Using fMRI, she observed the brain in real time, and discovered that changes to neural structure during meditation actually persist even after the person stops meditating.

For example, the amygdala, a region of the brain associated with memory and the processing of emotion, shows modestly dampened responses to emotive images when the person is a meditator versus when they aren't. This suggests that people who meditate may have learnt better emotional self-regulation. Currently, research is still ongoing to determine what exact aspects of meditation cause this effect and how we can use it in the treatment of depression and other mood disorders.

Some researchers have even found that mindfulness is associated with better relationships, and it's easy to imagine why. Barnes, Dekeyser, Wachs, and Cordova have all separately identified that mindfulness improves communication and strengthens a healthy response to relationship conflict and stress.

Finally, there have also been a few (admittedly small and inconclusive) studies which suggest that mindfulness may work as an intervention for physical conditions with a strong psychological component, such as irritable bowel syndrome, psoriasis, and fibromyalgia.

The research is strongly suggestive—there doesn't seem to be an area of life that isn't improved by adopting a more mindful approach. Tuning into the present moment with calm, non-judgmental awareness has been connected with greater insight, better immune functioning, stress management, faster cognitive speed, improved self-esteem, better intuition and even an enhanced sense of morality.

A Historical Perspective: From the East to the West, and from Religion to Science

Now that we've identified a straightforward working definition for mindfulness, and have seen that there's no shortage of evidence to support its benefits for our overall well-being, let's take a closer look at the history behind this now popular movement. In knowing where some of these concepts and practices have actually come from, we gain a deeper understanding and insight into their original purpose.

People have been cultivating mindfulness using various practices for thousands of years, but almost always as part of a greater cultural and historical tradition. **Broadly, mindfulness developed in an Eastern religious framework and was heavily influenced by the spiritual philosophies of both Hinduism and Buddhism.** Some have argued, though, that other religious traditions also have their own version of mindfulness, and that today the concept is truly international and secular.

Nevertheless, we can gain insight into the heart of mindfulness by understanding the spiritual institutions that primarily gave rise to mindfulness practices. Hinduism is the oldest surviving world religion (its earliest beginning being traced back 4000 years ago to the Indus Valley), and has been understood as a blend of many historical traditions throughout ancient India.

Key Vedic writings (for example the Bhagavad Ghita) were created around 3000 years ago and detail important stories and rituals, although these texts have been subsequently added to. A large part of the identity of Hinduism has always been mindfulness—in fact, reading some of these ancient texts is not all that different from reading a work by any of the modern mindfulness authors today.

Buddhism has also had a pronounced influence on our modern-day conception of mindfulness. Founded around 500 BCE by Gautama Buddha, Buddhism is fundamentally concerned with living in harmony with the fundamental laws of the universe, and seeking enlightenment from the constant round of karmic suffering. Over the course of hundreds of years, Buddhism spread throughout the East and split into different philosophical traditions, for example Japanese Zen and Tibetan Buddhism.

Throughout, the concept of mindfulness remained central. Today, many people in the West have their first introduction to the concept of mindfulness either via Western writings on Buddhism, or through a more accessible form: yoga.

Historically and culturally, yoga is inseparable from the practice of mindfulness. Bodily awareness can be cultivated in exactly the same way as awareness of external sensations or of one's thoughts or feelings. By focusing on the breath and its flow in the moment, yoga has been rightly described as a "moving meditation" and had been used as an adjunct to more traditional sitting meditation.

Today, meditation, mindfulness, and yoga are commonplace in the West, although practiced with a greater or lesser degree of faithfulness to the original tradition. With certain authors (such as Kabat-Zinn who founded Mindfulness Based Stress Reduction, or MBSR) and influential teachers and speakers (like Thích Nhất Hạnh) bringing mindfulness to the West, the concept is now thoroughly embedded in modern psychology and personal development literature everywhere.

Joe Kabat-Zinn is known as the father of secular mindfulness and has been largely responsible for popularizing the concept of mindfulness in the West for the last forty years. His MBSR courses essentially aim to offer Westerners the benefits of mindfulness… without the Buddhism.

Kabat-Zinn is himself not a Buddhist and wanted to emphasize instead the therapeutic benefits of mindfulness practice for everything from pain relief to stress management. Passionately believing that mindfulness is the medicine for much that ails the Western world, Kabat-Zinn has aggressively promoted mindfulness (some would say "McMindfulness") in everything from health care, to education, psychology, business, science, government and global politics.

Kabat-Zinn essentially sees the world as needing mindfulness more than ever—in an era of overpopulation, climate collapse, political instability and inequality, mindfulness could be the key to a saner, calmer, and more compassionate future.

Mindfulness from the Eastern Perspective

Hindus may find the West's emphasis on yoga as a trendy stress relief tool and fitness fad a little one-dimensional. For a traditional yogi or mindfulness practitioner, the idea of using mindfulness to enhance military training, improve athletic performance or be a better businessman is a little nonsensical.

Yoga was originally intended to be part of a comprehensive spiritual discipline and path, and was never practiced for its own end, but rather as something that allowed one to attain higher states of consciousness.

For the Hindus, mindfulness is only the first step, and something to assist in the ultimate aim: union with the divine.

From the Eastern perspective, holding awareness is just one of many mental skills to cultivate, and the others take considerably more discipline and dedication that go beyond a weekly yoga class. In training our thoughts to stay still and under our conscious control, we strengthen our awareness in much the same way as we strengthen various muscles through repeated, controlled actions during exercise. And much like how exercise should be done with a dedication to consistency before we see positive results, so too should mindfulness be practiced habitually before we reap its benefits across a wide range of contexts.

The Buddhist perspective, on the other hand, also differs, and is divided in itself across many varying disciplines and traditions, in many different countries. After all, 2500 years have passed since the teachings of the original Buddha—things were bound to have changed somewhat since then!

So, what does it mean for the novice interested in mindfulness that there are so many different traditions, both modern and ancient, Eastern and Western? Is it only possible to practice "real" mindfulness by being true to its ancient Eastern origins? Is one guru, speaker, author, or leader objectively better or more correct than another?

There are a plethora of different constructs, perspectives, theories, models, opinions, histories, ideas, and traditions associated with mindfulness—and the sheer volume of different paths can prove to be quite intimidating for someone starting out.

Acknowledging the value of compassion, non-attachment, and kindness, we can take a distinctly Buddhist approach and try to show respect to all unique paths, even if they're not our own. Each approach can be understood as a spoke on a great wheel held together by a central spike—though each spoke comes from a completely different direction, each points inwards to the same place, and ultimately serves a unified purpose.

As you explore mindfulness practice for yourself, or perhaps take up meditation, you may encounter various teachings, concepts, and theoretical underpinnings. The more historical and detailed metaphysical concepts are well beyond the scope of this introductory book, but for now, it may be enough to simply be aware of the presence of differences, and remain open to them without making any judgments yet about which is "correct." Keep in mind that despite such discrepancies, the core principles of mindfulness still hold and its essence remains the same—awareness of the present moment, without judgment.

Mindfulness is intensely private and experiential—your own practice is the arena for your learning and insight, and not the words of other people. Nevertheless, in the chapters that follow we will be working within a predominantly contemporary, Western understanding of mindfulness, which will differ from the countless other approaches you could potentially adopt.

Ultimately, we will be abandoning dogma to focus on the lived experience of better mental control, with a focus on boosting well-being in simple, practical, and achievable ways.

Mindfulness in the Modern Era, and Positive Psychology

Today, the modern Western reader is likely to encounter mindfulness concepts in self-help literature or in the general tenets of positive psychology. It's not surprising—both aim to improve mood, integrity, resilience, compassion, interpersonal connection, joy, and overall quality of life. No matter what relational or psychological issue you're dealing with, it's hard to imagine how a mindfulness practice would be inappropriate.

In the modern era, mindfulness can appear in many guises:

- As a self-care technique. Regularly taking time out to go still within yourself, breathe and re-center is a great way to take care of your mental health in a stressful, frantic world.
- As a way to increase workplace harmony and employee well-being. Mindfulness can tune us into our needs, as well as help us be compassionate with the needs of the people we work with.
- As a way to cope with stress and adversity. During a crisis, mindfulness can act as a rudder, helping us to stay resilient and deal with overwhelming situations with grace.
- As a tool for active stress relief. You could meditate before bed or use a mindfulness practice in a morning ritual to gather yourself for a busy day ahead.
- To manage challenges like depression and anxiety—mindfulness practices can work hand

in hand with therapy, especially CBT-style interventions.
- As a way to promote and support physical and spiritual wellness. Mindfulness can be built into a yoga practice or other exercise routine, and could even be used in conjunction with prayer, ritual, or journaling.

Mindfulness in the modern world may look rather different from how it did in ancient India, in the sociocultural context that the Buddha lived in. But that's OK! How you choose to use mindfulness concepts in your own life is entirely up to you.

Neuroscience on Mindfulness and Meditation: Why You Have "Two Minds"

Let's return to Norman Farb and colleagues at the University of Toronto, who you may recall from an earlier section. Their ground-breaking 2007 study, *Mindfulness meditation reveals distinct neural modes for self-reference,* looked at how human brains actually employ two separate neural networks when they interact with the world.

The first is the default network which is active when your external world is pretty quiet, but you're busy inside your head, ruminating, planning, worrying, and wondering. Farb called this the "narrative circuit" since it essentially tells stories, about ourselves, others, and the world. It's all about interpretations and meaningful connections. This circuit runs automatically and effortlessly.

The second circuit is called "direct experience," and it activates far more of your brain. Here, you are not thinking about the past or the future, or telling yourself a story, but experiencing the present moment via your sense organs, right as it unfolds.

Crucially, these two are *mutually exclusive*: stress about what you're going to make for dinner tonight and you miss how sweet the birds sound in the moment. But focus on their lovely singing and your narrative circuitry quiets down.

Narrative circuitry is useful for planning and strategizing, but **it's in direct experience that we actually encounter reality**, where we feel as though we are actually alive. This isn't to say that spending time in one state of consciousness is better than the other, but rather that it can be useful to make clear distinctions between them, and notice when you are in each state.

Say you're on vacation at a breathtaking beach. While you're seated on the shore in front of a magnificent sunset, you realize that the day is ending and think about the situation at the office you've left for the entire week. You start to worry. You wonder if the report you told your assistant to hand in has been submitted yet, you become anxious, and you plan what you'd do if your assistant hasn't followed through. This is the narrative circuit working. Yes, it might be useful to employ this type of thinking—if you're actually at the office and are required to accomplish such tasks.

But while you're at this beach, the narrative circuit does nothing but take you away from really savoring the scenery and appreciating the majesty of that sunset right in front of you. This is where and when you should be activating your direct experience circuit instead. Through this circuit, you can truly be in the moment, feeling the sand between your toes, smelling the exhilarating scent of your piña colada, and witnessing the wonderful sunset hues of the sky.

Note that the goal of mindfulness is not to totally eliminate the narrative circuit in your system. The trick is to be aware and in control of how you move between the narrative and the direct experience circuits—and as you may have guessed, people who meditate have had much more practice in doing precisely that.

Mindfulness in Plain English

Self-Awareness and Mindfulness

Mindfulness is essentially self-awareness.

This state of mind, this ability to tap into "direct experience" in the here and now, is the core of every mindfulness-based technique or practice. However, mindfulness itself isn't a technique or a practice. It's more like an attitude, a perspective, or a state of being.

In the next chapter, we'll be looking at exactly how you can bring more mindfulness into your everyday life, but for now, it's important to acknowledge that when we talk about mindfulness, we are pointing to a state of consciousness, and not any one particular technique, tradition, theory or worldview—in fact, all of this more appropriately belongs to the "narrative mind"!

Our modern world doesn't facilitate a mindful state of consciousness, and often actively prevents it. Rushing from one stressful moment to the next, running on autopilot and never truly connecting to the body, the breath or the moment as we inhabit it, we seem to wander the earth with vague existential complaints, a feeling of dissatisfaction, addiction to distraction, and the sense that life is passing us by.

An attitude of open, receptive awareness right here, right now, is the simplest but also most profound starting point to find better balance and contentment within ourselves. Mindfulness, then, is not so much a "what" as a "how."

The Pillars of Mindfulness

According to Joe Kabat-Zinn, there are seven basic pillars or attitudes that form the foundation of mindful living. These were first popularized in his bestselling book *Full Catastrophe Living*, but can be found in some form or other anywhere mindfulness is being discussed.

An attitude of non-judgment and non-attachment

Withhold judgment of what you are aware of. You don't need to analyze, interpret, or form an opinion. Just let things be as they are. Watch with calm, accepting impartiality. There is a constant stream of sensations within us—but we don't have to get caught up in them, or identify with or make meaning out of our every thought or feeling. Take a step back and withhold deciding whether something is liked or disliked, good or bad, expected or unexpected, and so on.

Beginner's mind

This term is often associated with Zen Buddhism, and it seeks to describe a kind of open receptivity, something like the new and fresh mind of a beginner who isn't yet stuck in the rut of believing he knows everything. Expertise and expectation can be a trap.

Instead try to see things anew, in every moment. Clear your mind and simply observe, as though you and your current experience had no history before that moment. Take the clutter out of your mind and you may see *what is*, rather than what you hope, expect, assume, and so on.

Patience

Impatience means anxiously waiting for a moment that comes at some other time than the present, some better moment in the future that hasn't yet arrived. Focusing on the present moment, on the other hand, reminds us to be patient—the now is the only place we will ever inhabit, after all!

Let things unfold at the pace they will. How could it be otherwise? Can we sit with what is, right now, rather than always wanting things to be different than how they are?

Trust

This means trust in both yourself and in the greater unfolding of which you are but a small part. Fully inhabit your own authority to have your own experience. Look within. What does your intuition say? The only person in this world who gets to be you is you—embrace it and own the fact.

Acceptance

This is easier said than done. Without any resistance, open up to and accept whatever emerges in the present moment. There is no need to force, change or deny what you become aware of.

Acceptance doesn't mean we condone what we encounter—it just means we fully acknowledge and sit with its existence without wanting to flee. For example, during meditation you may notice again and again that you are feeling irritated. Simply accept that this is the case, rather than trying to pretend you aren't, or that something else is happening.

Non-striving

There is no goal in meditation. Being mindful, we are not going anywhere or achieving anything. We are just being. There is nowhere to arrive—you are simply where you already are, and that's that.

Striving to be other than what you are right now is only another way of saying that you are unacceptable as you currently are. It's a way of denying the present—which is all you have! If you practice mindfulness only so that you can boost your ego, solve a problem, or just feel better… you are simply engaging in more "thought traffic." Just try to quietly observe the thought traffic instead.

Release into the flow

In the never-ending flow of thoughts and feelings that washes over our awareness every second of every day, we may notice that some ideas are particularly "sticky." We can get stuck on a nagging thought, a persistent memory, an unhappy worry, and so on.

On the other hand, we may dig in our heels and refuse to go fully into an experience that's beckoning. Whether we're extra-willing to experience some sensations or extra-reluctant to go along with others, we need to relax and let them both flow by, without trying to push or pull, hold on to or resist, in any way.

A Word of Warning

Before we dive into the next chapter, it's worth taking a moment to spell out a quick caveat where mindfulness is concerned. Though the potential benefits are enormous, it's fair to say that for now, the scientific evidence to support some claims is still largely inconclusive, and many key studies unfortunately suffer from rather poor methodology.

Over and above the research limitations, there are some conceptual limitations that we should also be cognizant of. The effort to reshape Buddhism so that it essentially aligns with Western science and philosophy has led to a heavy emphasis on the individual, and personal attainment. This is a far cry from the intention of the collectivist societies who originated these ideas, and who used them to go beyond the ego, not reinforce it.

Many traditional teachers take exception to the work of people like Joe Zabat-Kinn since they break mindfulness off from its religious roots and repackage and market it as a secular, rational, scientific and "universal" (i.e. Western) concept. Some purists worry that the watering down or downright falsification of certain mindfulness concepts has done more harm than good.

There have even been reports of people experiencing meditation-induced mania, anxiety, and psychosis, as well as some discovering that meditation reactivates traumatic memories (albeit at more intense meditation retreats).

This doesn't mean that meditation hasn't helped millions of people around the world, or that it can't help you. It does mean, however, that it's probably wise to proceed slowly at first and with modest expectations. In other words, let us try to explore the realm of mindfulness mindfully!

The Takeaway:

- Mindfulness is a quality of consciousness—the state of being aware of your experience in the present moment, without judgment.
- Mindfulness is not a fixed trait but an **attitude** that anyone can cultivate.
- While mindfulness and meditation are related concepts, they are not one and the same. Mindfulness is a state, while meditation is an activity. Through meditation, one can achieve a state of mindfulness.
- Mindfulness can help with all aspects of life, as it is not a specialized condition and is instead a state of awareness you can harness in each passing moment of your lived experience.
- Research has shed light on the numerous benefits of mindfulness. When engaged in consistently, mindfulness brings about an increased sense of calm, greater concentration and focus, reduced

stress levels, improved mood, better memory, and enhanced emotional regulation.
- Much of the modern secular philosophy of mindfulness has its roots in ancient Hindu and Buddhist tradition. Putting emphasis on cultivating awareness and acceptance as well as incorporating meditation in their rituals, both religions have the concept of mindfulness central to their practice.
- In the modern era, mindfulness has been a buzzword in positive psychology and self-help arenas, taking on a variety of forms including as a self-care technique, as a way to improve employee well-being, and as a tool for coping with stress, adversity, and emotional struggles.
- Neuroscience has pointed out that the brain has two separate neural networks: the "narrative circuit" which constantly tells stories and interprets our experiences, and the "direct experience circuit" which processes the present moment

through our sensory organs. One of mindfulness's benefits is to help us switch from the "narrative circuit" to the "direct experience circuit" so that we can achieve a heightened sense of awareness and calm in our daily life.
- The seven basic pillars of mindful living, as put forward by Joe Kabat-Zinn, are (1) an attitude of non-judgment and non-attachment, (2) beginner's mind, (3) patience, (4) trust, (5) acceptance, (6) non-striving, and (7) release into the flow.
- Note that some conceptual and research limitations exist as to the study of mindfulness's effects, so it's best to approach this practice slowly and with modest expectations—that is, take care to explore mindfulness mindfully.

Chapter 2. Everyday Mindfulness for Mental Calm

"Forever is composed of nows."

- *Emily Dickinson*

As we've already seen, mindfulness is not the same thing as meditation, although meditation is a practice that can facilitate and support mindfulness. We'll be looking at deliberate meditation exercises in a later chapter, but here, we'll consider a range of other techniques and practices that can help us experience more mindful states of awareness.

We don't need anything fancy to start—we start exactly where we are. In the now.

The ordinary activities of everyday life constitute the perfect arena on which to begin practicing mindfulness. Theoretically, as long as you have a brain and are alive, you can access a mindful state whenever, wherever.

Realistically, it can be a challenge at first to train yourself to hold a state of awareness that you might not be familiar with. The prospect of sitting down to "think of nothing" on a special cushion in the middle of your room may seem a little bizarre and daunting, but you don't have to begin with sitting meditation, or even use that method at all.

From the moment you wake up, your life is a parade of back-to-back invitations and opportunities to enter in a moment of conscious, heightened awareness.

As you wash your face, slow down and really feel the sensation of the water against your skin, and the smell of the soap. Eat your breakfast more slowly and notice not just the textures and tastes, but *yourself*, and how you feel. Completely relish the experience of having the chair support your weight underneath you.

There are many myths and misconceptions out there about what it means to be mindful. One of the most common is that you should be empty-minded, completely calm and serene, not allowing a single thought to puncture your flawless Zen perfection. Actually, this is a total fiction. Striving to reach this goal will likely only distract you further—and have you feeling bad for doing it wrong.

In truth, your mind *will* wander. Constantly.

Your job is not to rein your mind in like a naughty dog on a leash, but to simply watch it go. It doesn't matter that you get distracted or follow a narrative tunnel and temporarily forget that you were trying to stay in the moment. Simply notice what you are doing, and gently come back to the present. Again and again.

Ah, but maybe you notice yourself really messing up; you keep thinking of stuff you're not "supposed to," or your attention is split on all the millions of distracting sensations both internal and external. Maybe you think, "I suck at mindfulness, I have no self-discipline at all, I'm doing this really badly…"

That's fine too!

Notice these judgmental and critical thoughts as you would any other sensation. See them, and remind yourself not to be critical *of yourself being critical!* Relax, and accept the moment—all of it. Even if in the moment you simply find yourself bored, distracted, or irritated with something or other. If that is your experience in the moment, then that's what it is. Stay with it.

An interesting trick is to actively allow your mind to wander. What happens when you don't condemn yourself for not paying better attention? Try to bring yourself back again anyway. Observe that even a really strong and overwhelming emotion does something interesting after a while – it moves on.

The truth is that "perfect practice" is not sitting serenely, with nothing happening. Rather, it's being able to watch the near constant stream of thought traffic and understand it for what it is: transient and insubstantial.

The secret is that these thoughts and sensations *never stop*—they are a part of being alive. Rather, by practicing mindfulness you become better at being aware of them, and choosing whether you want to stumble along with them or stand to the side as they thrash around before giving way to the next sensation.

Notice judgment and boredom. Notice elation and peace. Notice stillness. Notice yourself coming back to the breath. Notice yourself wandering away from it again. Notice anger and fear, but also contentment. Relax and let it all be. Open up to the texture and tone of the present moment as it parades by without trying to change it, reject it, hold on to it, identify with it, analyze it or pass judgment on it.

Just allow your conscious awareness to shine a light on it, then let it pass.

Another persistent myth is that increased mindfulness is a sort of cheat code—a way to escape suffering and spare yourself getting affected by life's less pleasant aspects. But you may find, in practicing more mindfulness, that you are (obviously) aware of so much more in life—including the negative parts!

You might discover some previously hidden thoughts and feelings that are quite distressing. You may notice things that you previously avoided or ignored. Often, it's when the mind is still that things you have long kept deep in the ocean of your subconsciousness bubble up to the surface. But here, too, we need to be kind and compassionate, with ourselves and the very reality we inhabit. Try to see that your consciousness is not actually damaged or destroyed by the experience of pain—that you can hold pain, fear, and unpleasantness just as you can hold joy and ease and contentment.

What can help is to remind yourself that you are not actually striving for a goal. Just being aware. And if you discover you are not being aware, well, congratulations, your discovery shows that you have suddenly become aware. So, there's no problem. Just remain in that state of awareness. There is no need to strive, to force or to try extra hard to perform correctly.

So, you can be mindful as you wash dishes in the evening. You feel the soap suds. You are aware of a tightness in your lower back and a feeling of irritation. You watch the story you tell yourself, a story of being wronged at work that day, replete with good guys and bad guys, with plenty of anger and resentment and a sense of injustice. You watch as the story fades away again. You come back to the soap suds and the glossy reflection of the window that each and every one has on its surface…

A meditation bell is something that reminds you to stay aware in the present—and if you like, you can program any activity in your day as a meditation bell of sorts, a reminder to stop, take a few deep breaths, and find a center within yourself. You can make a habit of observing a few minutes of mindful silence before you switch activities, for example before you start the work day or when you end it, before you begin a meal, or after you complete a workout.

This technique fits mindfulness practice around the natural ebbs and flows of your day, and reminds you that it's not something special you do for an hour a day in a cloud of incense, but is instead a part of the fabric of your lived, conscious experience. It touches everything because it *is* everything.

You can maintain a sense of awareness in the middle of an activity, too. Do this by reminding yourself as often as you can to "check in" with the present moment. This may be nothing more than closing your eyes, taking a breath, and doing a scan of your body and mind. Remember, you're not trying to catch yourself out or make sure that you're having the "right" thoughts—you are simply waking up to the present, and reminding yourself that you can be here, now, in the moment, directly experiencing it.

Be mindful as you cook and eat, as you chat or listen, as you walk the dog or wait in line at the supermarket. There's a reason that so many meditation and mindfulness teachers focus on the breath—it's because it's always there as an "anchor" into the present moment.

Your breath is the exchange between you and the outside world. It's your life, and it's constantly moving, flowing in and out. Don't control it, just become aware of it as it moves through you. If you can do nothing but become more aware of your breath and how it enters and leaves your body, you will have mastered an incredibly profound practice that some masters devote their lives to.

Your body is also an anchor, because it can never be anywhere else except the present. As long as your awareness is hooked into sensory perception (from your eyes, ears, nose, tongue, and skin), then you are in the direct experience circuit and not the narrative circuit.

As you practice more and more, every day, you will notice that you are at liberty to expand and contract your awareness at will. You can narrow it right down and zoom in on the texture of the ink of a single letter on a page, for example, or you could open up wider to allow in sensations from all your senses, as well as internal feelings and thoughts. You may notice that you can shift your conscious attention, placing it on the external one moment and the internal the next.

A great way to be more mindful is to do so in interactions with others. When you talk to another person, really be present with them, completely. Listen with all of yourself, without thinking of what you'll say next, without jumping in to offer an opinion, to decide if you agree or disagree, and so on. Just immerse yourself in their world for a moment.

Pause, take a breath, and then respond. As you express yourself, be fully present, too. Take your time to inhabit each and every moment to its fullest, without distraction.

Can you just see the person in front of you as they are, without telling yourself a story about the purpose or meaning behind the moment you are sharing? Can you both be together, in this unfolding present, without force or analysis or rushing onto the next thing? If you can bring more mindfulness to your social interactions, you may notice an incredible boost in your own intuition and powers of perception—and you may suddenly find people far more interesting that you thought they were!

Bring mindfulness to your commute. You don't have to do yoga to be mindful during exercise—stay present and aware during any exercise, including simple stretching or just going for a walk. Notice the world around you or the sensation of the millions of tiny motions your body makes to move you smoothly from this moment to the next.

Bring mindfulness to the table—eat slowly and with full awareness of the tastes, textures, and aromas of your meals. Allow your mind to immerse in the experience. If you eat more slowly, you may also discover that you are satisfied with so much less food, yet enjoy it more. It will be easier to naturally stop overeating or mindlessly guzzling junk food that you don't even really enjoy.

No matter what you do throughout the day, inject a little bubble of conscious awareness into it. Notice that, when you more consciously attempt to be present, even ordinary days can seem so much fuller and richer. In a way, they are, *because you're finally there and present to actually experience it all.* You may find so much joy and peace in the simplest of things, and find your stress levels drop as you move away from rumination and distraction.

Reading, Writing, and Listening Mindfully

Like most people in the world today, you probably spend a lot of your time taking in or processing information in the form of reading or listening. Whether you're a student at school, an entrepreneur or employed full time, you likely spend much of your day *learning*. Even when we're not working or studying, we read and browse the internet, or watch TV, or learn a new skill or hobby.

Mindfulness can be brought to all these activities.

It's no exaggeration to say that the world is flooded with information, which basically rushes at us at full speed from the moment we wake up. If we use our brains mindlessly and without awareness, we are missing out on an opportunity to synthesize, store and integrate this information more efficiently. If we are mindful, however, we give ourselves a crucial window in which our brains can actually learn—not just be bombarded with data, but properly digest it.

When we are not mindful in our learning process, we risk getting carried away unawares, never truly practicing proactive discernment for the material we take in, or why, or what we do with it. When we can stand aside and clearly see how our brains are working, we are always better positioned than if we were just passively going along with the next thought or sensation. **By being mindful, we take ownership of our mental faculties.**

While we've focused somewhat in this book on how mindfulness can improve emotional self-regulation, it can also improve our intellectual and cognitive functions. Any time we employ our mental faculties to write, read or listen to new information, we can practice being mindful and present.

Mindful Reading

Why read? Is it because you want to get to the last page as quickly as possible? Or just to find the nuggets of information you need for a book report? Approaching reading as a chore to rush through or a means to an end can actually be counterproductive.

When we read mindfully, we are not concerned with cramming as much info into our brains as possible, as quickly as possible. Instead, we give ourselves ample time to pause, reflect, and absorb what we've read. Merely running your eyes along the page and understanding the meaning of the letters and words is "reading" in a sense… but you can do better.

When you are mindful, you provide a space for profundity and insight to bloom. You spend time together, just you and the text, in the moment. You don't rush, and you don't assume you already know what's being said. You allow the deeper meaning of the words to emerge, at its own pace.

You may like to begin and end every reading session with a few moments spent sitting quietly with your breath. Relax your mind and notice how you're feeling in the moment. When you're done reading, pause again to allow things to settle. You are not doing "nothing"—you are actively creating space for your mind to soak up what it's encountered.

Take your time. Do you really like a particular sentence or phrase? Linger on it and savor it as you would a delicious meal. Get in close to feel its rhythm, the way it uses language, the images and emotions it evokes for you. When you pause, you give your mind time to take everything in, arrange it, and synthesize it with your existing knowledge. This takes reading and transforms it from a joyless data-transfer process to a richer and more dynamic dialogue, an experience of real communication.

You don't need to do any of this alone, either. When a group of people mindfully read the same poem or piece of literature, there are suddenly multiple, enriching perspectives to reflect off one another. A mindful reading group could have someone read aloud, slowly, while others focus and listen. You might be amazed to find that hearing things spoken in different voices suddenly changes their texture and the feelings they evoke.

Mindful Writing

Writing is seldom considered when people talk about mindfulness, but it's a human activity that can be immensely improved by committing to really perceiving things *as they are*, fresh and new to the senses each time. Mindfulness can teach us a lot about being better writers. We sharpen our capacity to bear witness, to hold all of life's expression, not just the pleasant or easy parts. Being mindful, we simply notice more, and can more faithfully document it.

In a conscious state, we become more skillful in our thinking process, more deliberate, concise, discriminating. We open up to more. And where the writing process itself is concerned, we learn to watch it all unfold, without expectation. We become more agile in switching perspectives, and can be more patient as a work takes it time coming into being.

Simply writing in a journal is an easy, accessible way to practice mindfulness. You don't need to be a professional writer to care about mindful writing—meditation and poetry are perfectly complimentary. Whichever side of the practice you are more interested in developing, a dabble with the other is likely to be enriching.

Journaling is a blend of expression and self-exploration. A journal is not for publication, and not for others to read. It's only there for you to enjoy the feeling of "putting your thoughts down" on the page, where you can cultivate your own experience of the moment, express your creativity, explore themes and ideas, or notice patterns when you step back and watch yourself thinking and writing.

How you use journaling as a mindfulness aid is precisely up to you. You can try "zen doodling"—just watch your pen trace along the page with no intention for where it will go. Or try to write automatically, as though the words want to write *you*, and you're reading them for the first time. Don't think too hard about any of it!

If you can journal daily, you give yourself the gift of seeing something marvelous: your changing consciousness, over time. The ebbs and flows, the fleeting nature of life's comings and goings—how day to day you are essentially always the same, and yet somehow never the same.

Use journaling to note down the things you are grateful for. Write love letters to the beautiful sunset you were gifted that evening. Jot down dreams, questions, knotty issues you're working through, reflections, pretty turns of phrase, ideas. Or you can simply turn up to the page every day, with no prior intention, and begin randomly with these words at the top of the page: "Here and now..." Then complete the sentence as it occurs to you, there and then.

Isn't it marvelous how many different things play out on this simple stage we call the present moment?

Some people practice "morning pages"—the habit of writing first thing in the morning, even before they get out of bed. Simply wake up, and commit to free writing loosely for a set time, for example fifteen minutes. It's like a release of everything that's built up in your head overnight. Don't think too hard, re-read anything, or pause at all. Just write whatever comes to you, quickly and without judgment. You may find this is a remarkable way of tapping into your inner experiences, gaining insight into your life, and heightening your own sense of identity and awareness.

Other people use their journals as their own personal gurus: they write down their burning questions or quandaries… and then answer them themselves. This dialogue can be an incredibly effective way of gaining clarity and insight into life's challenges. It's a way of externalizing and slowing down the decision-making process, helping you bring deliberate awareness and organization to your thinking.

Use mindfulness even when you're doing more mundane writing. Take your time to write your shopping list in beautiful colored calligraphy, choose thoughtful and kind words in your emails, or start a practice where you breathe quietly and meditate for a few minutes before deciding to write anything on social media.

Mindful Listening

Finally, information can also find its way to us in the form of the spoken word. Unfortunately, modern life encourages one-way conversations—we speak out into the void that is social media or passively watch others on TV, unable to really connect with or respond meaningfully to what is shared with us.

Mindful listening is a radical way to bring deep, authentic presence to the act of someone else's expression.

Attention is at a premium in our noisy, info-saturated world. If you think about it, it can be a tremendous act of respect and generosity to give someone your complete, undivided attention. Aren't we all craving the very same kindness and consideration from others?

Can you listen with no assumptions, and no inner voice insisting on talking back, arguing or stating its own agenda? Listening is about an overall willingness to be perceptive and receptive—but this does not mean adopting a weak, passive position! Rather, we go quiet within ourselves so that we can receive another—their voice, their ideas, their emotions, their reality, their perspective.

We remain calm, alert, and open, accepting their being as an expression of the present moment.

When we meditate, we say to every sensation that emerges in the stream of the present: "Hello, I see you. I accept you with compassion." When we listen mindfully, we extend this same attitude to those experiences and perceptions that go beyond our own world, our own ego, and our own expectations. We witness another and allow ourselves to temporarily and respectfully enter their field of consciousness, *sharing the moment* with them.

Want to be a more mindful listener? Try cutting down on the noise in your life.

Regularly turn off things that bleep and hum in the background, and switch off TVs and radios you're not really listening to. When you wake up in the morning or last thing before you sleep, let your ears savor the sounds of nature outside, the chatter of distant people or traffic, or simply silence (it *does* have a sound!). Let your conscious awareness sink fully into every sensation, without labeling anything as good or bad.

Another practice is to deliberately use sound to focus your attention in the present. Music (and in particular prayer and chanting) has been used for millennia to repeatedly pull the mind back from wandering and into the fullness of the present moment. As you might recall from the previous discussion about the narrative circuit and the direct experience circuit, these two modes of thinking are mutually exclusive.

Choose soothing and pleasant music you enjoy and focus entirely on it. Listen to every tone and harmony, and draw your attention to the sensations that emerge in your heart, mind, and body as you listen. If your thoughts wander, gently come back again, as you would with any other mindfulness practice.

Finally, a perfect way to practice mindful listening is to fully attend to the people who talk to you, even if it's just in ordinary, everyday conversation. Focus only on what they are expressing. Notice their facial features and how they move and shift, the timbre and volume of their voice, their posture, their hand movements, the words they're using... even what they're not saying.

Forget about your own story for a moment, and try not to immediately start thinking of a response, rebuttal or compliment. You have plenty of time to formulate your own response when the other person is completely finished speaking.

Sometimes, the art of good conversation starts with one or both participants willingly slowing down, tuning out distractions and making a space for real connection to happen. You may find that your own full presence acts as an unspoken invitation to the other person to do the same.

Most of our days are filled with an abundance of opportunities to listen closely and with attention. There's always a brand-new chance to fully engage with the words around us, not merely to quickly rush to their end, but to appreciate them and what they represent, right there in the moment.

The stressed-out, ruminating, and overthinking mind uses language too, however. You might find that reading certain material or engaging in certain kinds of conversation is the very trigger that spurs mindlessness. But luckily, all you need to do is to become aware that this is happening, even if only for the briefest moment. Then, commit to using language mindfully instead.

As you go about your day, watch yourself and how you use your words, where your attention falls, how you speak about the world, yourself, and others. Notice the effect that certain people, ideas or even social media platforms have on you. In many ways, we live in a world of words—stories, narratives, opinions, and arguments surround us on all sides.

But we can always bring a little more awareness into how we move through it all, the roles we play, how we express ourselves, and what we choose to focus on. We can always use both awareness and discernment to cultivate lives that feel good to us.

Maybe, through mindfulness, you notice how often you use the word "hate" in ordinary speech. Maybe you see that a close friend and yourself always seem to have the same conversation, over and over again. Maybe you realize that your best conversation partner is actually the person who says the least when you're together!

Whatever emerges in your present moment, by acknowledging and accepting it fully, as it is, you take the first step to consciously changing it. If you want to, that is.

Keeping a Mindfulness Journal

We can become mindful anytime we write something. But we can also specifically dedicate a journal to mindfulness practice alone. The idea is to slow down your thoughts and put them out into the world, onto paper. Once expressed, these thoughts are easier to process and, if you like, release.

Again, journaling of all kinds can be therapeutic and meditative, but there are ways to be more deliberate, and use a journaling session as a focused mindfulness practice that goes beyond just putting pen to paper. Firstly, decide what format will work best for you—a "digital journal" on an iPad, a simple Word processor, a beautiful hardback paper journal that you write in with a fountain pen, or simply loose paper that you discard when you're done.

It's up to you entirely, but be aware that digital devices may encourage distraction, and, some would argue, simply don't offer the same immersive experience as pen and paper. Similarly, you don't need a journal with written prompts inside—blank pages are fine. Most people find that selecting a special journal they love and use exclusively for the purpose helps them focus and appreciate the ritual of the practice.

Once you've found the right journal, then what? What do you write?

Below are some writing prompts to get you started, but if you spend a few quiet moments before writing, you'll likely find that you can come up with plenty of interesting threads on your own.

- What state of mind/feeling/thoughts do I want to cultivate today? How do I want to **be** today?
- What am I grateful for today?
- What has felt beautiful, alive, and poignant for me today?
- How am I feeling? Can I look at all the sensations of my body, heart, and mind openly, and without judgment?
- What can I let go of today?
- What do I need today? What are my desires?
- What is bubbling into awareness today? Do I have any questions, concerns, or threads I'd like to follow?
- What happened today and how do I feel about it?

- What are my intentions for the day ahead?

While it is important to remain focused and purposeful as you write, try to remember that there is no right or wrong way to do this. Think of your journaling as externalized meditation. Write on any of the above prompts for ten minutes at least. You might like to dwell on the words for a moment afterwards, or even return to writing if it feels right.

Remember, you are working with your own consciousness—notice what you are noticing. Become curious about your state of mind, or the state of your bodily experience, as you express yourself. Notice how some elements are coming more into awareness—if you date your entries, you can even see how certain themes, ideas, and feelings evolve over time.

With time, you can write without prompts, trusting yourself to feel into awareness where it's needed. Do what works for you! Just avoid using a journal to externalize mindless rumination, and avoid turning it into a dispassionate and unconscious list of events, or automatic and spontaneous responses that remain unexamined.

A mindfulness journal can deepen insight and help you cultivate self-awareness, but it's also fantastic at enhancing creativity. Art is only improved with more curiosity, and genuine attention. Sink into the details, into the essence of things. Really *feel* them. Touch the ineffable.

Take a walk outside in nature for twenty minutes and return to express your experience, documenting and relishing the sensations, the insights. Be creative. You could also use your journal to revisit old memories, entering into them in body and mind to process and release them. However you choose to use your journal, what's important is that you're consistent—try setting aside some time every day for quiet journal reflection, so that journaling becomes a habit.

The Takeaway:

- Meditation is not the same as mindfulness, which can be practiced right now, no matter what you are doing. Each day presents opportunities to enter a state of heightened awareness, in the ordinary activities that you engage in—from washing your face, to eating, to the daily commute, to your interactions with others.

- A common myth about the practice of mindfulness is that it requires total emptiness of the mind, where every emerging thought is blocked by a wall to prevent it from disturbing a pure, flawless Zen state. In reality, however, the mind **will** wander—and you are not required to completely stop it from doing so.
- In mindfulness, you can allow your mind to wander, and work instead toward simply becoming aware, notice the stream of thoughts without becoming attached to it, and anchor back to the now. All you need is an attitude of non-striving, acceptance, patience, and the willingness to consistently and gently bring yourself back to the present.

- A way to come back to the present moment is to tune in to your breathing. As the breath remains constant no matter what time of the day it is or what activity you engage in, breathing is a natural anchor you can use to bring yourself back to the now. Focusing on how your breath moves in and out of you leads you to redirect your consciousness to what is in the here and now.
- In addition to breathing, your body's sense perceptions (from your eyes, ears, nose, tongue, and skin) are effective anchors you can employ to activate your direct experience circuit instead of your narrative circuit.
- You can be mindful when you interact with others. As you talk with the person in front of you, really see them, be fully with them, and immerse yourself in their world for the time that you are with them.
- Practice mindfulness as you read, write, and listen. Mindful reading allows a space for absorption,

reflection, and insight to boom. Mindful writing sharpens your capacity for keen observation, discernment, and faithful documentation of what is. Mindful listening grants you the ability to remain calm, open, and accepting of the other person's being as an expression of the present moment.

Chapter 3. Melding Mindfulness with Meditation

"Meditation is not a way of making the mind quiet. It is a way of entering into the quiet that is already there—buried under the 50,000 thoughts the average person thinks every day."

- *Deepak Chopra*

Meditation for Novices and Veterans

We already know that mindfulness is not the same as meditation, but for most purposes, it's useful and convenient to think about mindfulness in terms of a meditation practice. To define it simply, **meditation is any mental practice involving three key features: awareness, focus, and relaxation.** Though we can find these three experiences in a range of different activities, meditation is the *deliberate pursuit of all three*.

Usually done quietly and alone in a seated position, with eyes closed, we can expand meditation to include the more popular, psychology-based perspective, wherein we become more familiar with our inner cognitive and psychological processes. This means we can use meditation to become more aware of and skilled at things like concentrating, or observing neutrally without attachment.

This definition may sound simple, but due to its intangible and personal nature, meditation has often been misunderstood, and myths abound about what counts as meditation. Firstly, don't believe that you need to wear certain clothes, burn incense, sit on a special cushion or play whale song in the background. The only requirement is that you are still and undisturbed—

although that doesn't mean you can't meditate if there are dogs barking in the distance or noisy neighbors upstairs!

You don't need to be a Buddhist or include any particular religious or spiritual elements in your meditation practice—unless you want to, of course. There are people who will go to great lengths to make meditation seem like a very exclusive club, or suggest that you need decades of practice before you can even be considered a beginner. This is nothing more than ego.

In fact, many of the myths associated with meditation are ego-based. In truth, there's no need to make any grand changes to your identity just because you practice meditation. You are not betraying your chosen religion, or committing to a life of an ascetic monk or a new-age spiritualist. You're just meditating, and *anyone* can meditate. You don't need a master, a guru or a month-long retreat that costs you thousands (although, again, there's nothing to stop you doing these things if you want to).

Some people look at meditation and see nothing but avoidance—it seems selfish to them, to sit around doing "nothing" while there's real work to be done. By the time you're done reading this book, you'll hopefully see that meditation is one of the most valuable ways to spend your time, and, rather than being escapist and selfish, it actually encourages an embracing of reality, and a deep compassion for self and others.

Though meditation can lead to relaxation, it is *not* the same as simply chilling out (as valuable as chilling out is!). Relaxation is an effect of meditation, but not strictly its method. Similarly, using affirmations, visualizations, trance, or self-hypnosis may be beneficial, but these things encourage a wholly different state of mind than does meditation. There are many different states of consciousness—to simply alter consciousness (for example through psychedelics) is not the same as meditation.

Finally, though meditation is not effortless (after all, you are trying to focus and concentrate on the present moment, which is by definition effortful), it is not in itself difficult. You are not meant to be fighting against yourself, or forcing your mind to clear. Yes, the process can seem daunting/boring/confusing to a beginner, but it's something anyone can do with practice—even those of us who feel we don't have the time, or are more distractible than others.

As you learn more about what meditation is and how it feels, you may encounter your own biases and misconceptions about it. Try to keep an open mind, though, and be receptive to learning more.

Mindfulness Is Not Synonymous with Meditation

We've already seen that mindfulness and meditation are not exactly the same thing. But if there are so many benefits to simply being more mindful, what's the point of taking up meditation as well? Though experts and gurus of all stripes have debated the issues extensively, the truth is probably that they are two overlapping and complimentary paths to well-being.

Mindfulness is a state of awareness, which can be cultivated using the technique or practice of meditation. However, some people claim that meditation is an umbrella term that encompasses mindfulness, itself a form of meditation, along with other forms like yoga, tantra, mindful breathing, contemplating emptiness, visualization, etc.

Being mindful, we bring our full attention and awareness to a single thing—the present moment or our breath, for example. Though mindfulness can be used during meditation, meditation can employ a range of other techniques and work toward a variety of different ends. Mindfulness is a little like the ability to run, whereas meditation encompasses all the different forms of sports—many of which require running.

Why meditate? Well, you don't have to. There are benefits to simply being more mindful. However, a meditation practice can take you a little further. Whether you want to tap into the deepest secrets of being itself and reach divine union, enlightenment and the dissolution of your illusory ego, or you simply want to relax a little and be more emotionally balanced, meditation and mindfulness can help, depending on how they're used.

Types of Meditation—Which Would Work Best for You?

So that leads us to the next obvious question—which type of meditation should you practice?

It's not enough to simply sit cross-legged, close your eyes and dive in with no sense of purpose or direction. It makes sense to choose an approach that actually fits *your* needs and goals.

To determine what those goals are, ask yourself: What's missing from your life right now?

How are you in general—how is your body, how is your mind? Do you have tense muscles, overactive, racing thoughts or trouble tempering your emotions?

What do you hope to really achieve from meditation—energy, focus, purpose, insight, healing?

Assessing where you are right now will help you better decide which form of meditation to pursue first. Most beginners usually benefit from a more secular, contemporary approach with clear goals and a structure to stick to. Some of these approaches include:

Guided meditation

This is what it sounds like—there is a recorded voice or a live teacher who leads you through a structured meditation session. Typically, you will be asked to focus on either visualizations, or to concentrate on your breath or a part of your body as you relax. Guided meditations are often themed, and they can be great for beginners since they are a fixed length.

They're perfect for people just starting out who want to get the meditation ball rolling, and can improve well-being and focus, while building discipline with regular practice.

Loving-kindness meditation

In this meditation, you direct your conscious awareness to one specific aim: generating feelings of compassion and loving kindness toward yourself, others, and the world at large. This kind of meditation can be profoundly healing and completely change your world when done regularly. Improving not only social relationships but your ability to have self-compassion, this form of meditation is a great fit for people wanting to heal emotional wounds and cultivate empathy.

Mantra meditation

It can be difficult and confusing for some to "concentrate on the moment" but more intuitive to dwell on a repeated, often meaningless spoken phrase to continually refocus the mind. Any sound or word, if repeated, can be a tool to gently anchor in the present, and it may be a wonderful way for some people to structure a meditation practice. If you've ever seen those monks, often depicted in the media, repeatedly saying "om" at regular intervals, then you have an idea of what mantra meditation looks like.

Breathing meditation

The same effect can be achieved by using the breath. By staying with your breath, you stay in the moment, and strengthen your mind-body connection—great for people who have difficulty with rumination and anxiety. Breathing meditation can be wonderfully grounding and can clear the mind.

Mindfulness meditation

Here, we consciously practice becoming aware of what emerges in our present reality without judgment or attachment. We stay in the moment, and when we become aware of our attention wandering to the past or the future, or into a mental story, we calmly release it and come back to the present instead. This kind of meditation increases focus and decreases emotional reactivity, helping us gain a deeper sense of awareness and self-regulation. You may need to set a timer to remind you when your session is over.

A Mindful Framework

Mindfulness meditation is a popular and wonderful practice to choose as a beginner. You may be tempted to jump right in and start straight away, but take the time to lay the groundwork before beginning in earnest—this way you're less likely to get disheartened, bored or irritated and stop before you've had the chance to progress.

First decide *when* you'll practice. It's best to have a routine. Any time will work as long as it's a time of day where you're relatively free of distractions and can devote time and energy to practice. Ten minutes at first is more than enough, and you can practice after a daily exercise or yoga routine.

Next, decide *where* you'll practice. You don't need over-the-top hippie décor—you just need a peaceful, quiet place away from distractions. Set your timer, switch off your phone, tell people in your household you'll need some time to yourself and then start. If it helps, a little yoga to warm up can get you in the right frame of mind, as can a gentle walk, a journal session, a little prayer or ritual, or even some light music.

When you're ready, find your seated position—stable but not straining. There's no need for a super erect, uncomfortable posture. On the floor or in a chair is great. Settle in for a moment, finding comfort and balance. Keep your upper arms parallel to the rest of your body, palms on your upper thighs (no need for hand positions). Keep your chin slightly lowered, eyes closed or gaze gently downward without any focus.

Now, be there. Relax. Become aware of your breath, and follow it as it moves in and out of your body. Feel the slight friction of the air as it enters your nostrils. Note the soft rise of your chest, the warmth of the breath, the silence in your ears.

Whether it's within a single second or it takes five minutes, your mind will likely wander. Your awareness may jump to an unanswered email, to an event that happened yesterday morning, to the hunger in your stomach, to a vague feeling of apprehension floating around your lower belly... that's OK. Let it go and come back to the breath, to the present.

Rather than an attitude of judgment, have a little moment of gratitude that you came back to the moment, then let that gratitude go as well. It's all grist for the mill. If you feel an itch, pause and put your awareness there. Withhold scratching it or readjusting yourself. Can you just stay with the sensation, as it is?

When you're done, come out of meditation slowly and gently. Reconnect to your environment, and notice how you feel, inside and out. Don't just jump back into the day—reflect on *how* you'd like to continue. The more you practice, the more you will start to see the boundary between meditating and not meditating disappear.

Things to Keep in Mind about Meditation

It bears repeating—you don't need to *buy* anything to begin meditating. Not a special cushion, not bells or worry beads, not a fancy course or retreat or app. The only 100 percent necessary thing is you, and the present moment—which you already have!

Keep in mind that the goal is not to empty your head entirely, and that wandering thoughts are not a sign that you're weak, or out of practice, or doing it wrong. In fact, this is exactly what mindfulness meditation feels like. Embrace the present without judgment—*all* of the present, whatever it looks like. Even if the present is just you judging yourself, or you being distracted and tired. Even if it's just your brain wondering when you'll give it something more interesting to do.

Gravity isn't an enemy of your workout, and likewise your brain wandering around isn't an enemy of your meditation practice. It's just what brains do. But you are not your brain alone.

It's OK to not enjoy the occasional practice, to feel frustrated or like you're not "progressing." But to help yourself out, don't try to meditate when you're physically, mentally, or emotionally exhausted. Don't meditate with a full belly. Wear clothing that is comfortable and make sure that no devices are beeping or chiming during your session.

Challenges and Obstacles with Mental Chatter

It's perfectly normal for things not to go quite according to plan at first. Don't let a little snag in the beginning convince you that you're not cut out for meditation, and stop entirely. You may just need to do some troubleshooting.

Firstly, don't worry if you're shocked by just how uncontrollable and unruly your mind is! Don't freak out and attempt to *stop* these thoughts—remember, your only goal is to notice, without judgment or interpretation.

Being caught up in a frenzied mess of thoughts can feel like a seductive trance you can't help but slip into. But when you do, just slip out of it again. Watch and see that even though thoughts come, they also fade away. You're not doing anything wrong.

Notice the planning, fantasizing, worrying, analyzing, interpreting, storytelling, judging, questioning… Just be there, and be aware of it.

Notice if you are grasping at something, wanting to be somewhere other than the moment, wanting to escape or deny what's in front of you. Notice how you may push certain sensations away in anger or fear, or jump toward others to cling to them in desperation or excitement. Watch to see if you feel sleepy, irritable, restless, or doubtful. Are you asking yourself, "Is this even working?"

A great way to approach all of these challenges is not to see them as problems at all. They're simply part of the experience; a universal human experience. What happens when you *don't* try to control, resist or judge? Your attention can go to what is arising, without identifying with it. You can name it—fear, anger—without getting lost in it or stuck in its thought spirals.

A key principle to keep in mind is that you are not your thoughts. Any thought could occur in your mind, but it does not follow that you have to believe every thought you think, or that you have to act on every idea that floats in your head. When a thought comes, you can simply stand aside and observe as it passes by, as if watching a cloud float across the otherwise blue skies. As you master the art of beholding your thoughts in this way, you are saved from being carried away by destructive urges and emotions. You become better at simply letting things be, instead of trying to control or judge everything that happens to you. **You get to meet all experiences with compassionate attention. Then you are able to let them go.**

If you have experienced a great trauma, it may not be advisable initially to stay with very intense or powerful emotions as they emerge. Some traumas are so severe that they evoke emotions unmanageable by meditative practices alone. Such adverse experiences need to be processed through trauma work with a trained mental health professional before you can safely hold these emotions by yourself.

If for any reason you begin to feel intensely uncomfortable or overwhelmed by emotions during meditation, it may make more sense to place attention on something calming and compassionate instead of staying with the emotion. If you feel like you may be descending into panic or becoming disconnected from your body, anchor into the present moment using the 54321 grounding technique: Look around you and identify five things that you see, four things that you feel, three things that you hear, two things that you smell, and one thing that you taste (or if you find this difficult, one good thing about yourself).

Mindfulness meditation is about full, open awareness—but be patient and compassionate with yourself. It sometimes takes time to bear witness to emotions, memories, sensations, thoughts or parts of ourselves that are distressing. Focus awareness on a soothing image, a person you love, or a mantra that reaffirms your safety and well-being.

Finally, what about all those more mundane distractions—i.e. that wildly annoying feeling of your legs going to sleep, or a tiny mosquito buzzing around your ears?

The sad fact is, most of us are not used to sitting up straight, unsupported. Cramps, itching and numbness might happen. On the other hand, previously ignored sensations may come flooding to the fore. In the past, you might have been able to push away such sensations because you've been operating on autopilot and often get powered up by adrenaline in these busy times. However, now that you inject mindfulness in your life and take time to be still and observe, a heightened awareness of your body can make you aware of just how tired or unwell you feel.

Here's the trick: *any* sensation, be it mental, emotional, physical, or spiritual, can be dealt with in the same way: with compassionate awareness. We can sit with and accept unpleasant physical sensations just as we can emotional or mental ones. Just offer gentle attention. Breathe into it.

Be kind to yourself and open up a space to experience what you are experiencing. Notice what springs up in you in response to a physical sensation—can you see a whole cascade of inner thoughts and feelings that erupt over a simple leg itch?

Meet these with kindness and non-attachment, too.

You could direct your attention to something else if physical discomfort is really weighing on you. Be present with the feeling of unpleasantness—try not to immediately flee the sensation (but then again, there's nothing wrong with "giving up" and shifting position, or ending the session). Just remind yourself that all these sensations are fleeting. Put a little distance between you and doubt, discomfort, or rumination. Discomfort in a part of your body or doubt entering your mind are all part of you, but they are not you—hence, you can retain a consciousness that is not bothered or irritated by these sensations, but one that is able to hold and accept them as they come.

The Most Probable Culprits of Meditation Troubles

There's nothing wrong with experiencing worry, rage, irritation, doubt, lack of motivation, restlessness, impatience, low mood, or even falling asleep while you try to meditate. It's normal to get carried away with planning something else, trying too hard and getting frustrated, or finding it impossible to care enough to stick with it.

That being said, there are a lot of meditation mistakes that will make it so much more likely that you'll experience these kinds of challenges.

The most common is simple: your practice is not consistent. Strive to be consistent with meditating daily. You don't need to worry about allotting a huge chunk of your day to sitting on the floor and closing your eyes as you immerse yourself in meditative practice. The length of time you sit is of secondary importance to the regularity of your practice. Your mind is churning around constantly, 24/7. For a meditation practice to have any noticeable effect, it needs to be frequent enough to make a difference. Knowing this, have some discipline. If your day is jam-packed with task after task on your to-do list, sit for only two or three minutes—it's better than nothing.

Practice with commitment and intention. Have respect for yourself and your practice, and give it the time and intensity it deserves—sloppiness or lack of effort is a disservice to yourself. Meditation is not just some boring thing on your to-do list, so don't treat it like one! Prepare well before each session and give it the care and consideration it deserves. Set your intention, take some breaths, and ease into it.

Related to this is simply expecting too much, too soon. It took you a lifetime to be what you are right now—you will not magically achieve radical changes within a few weeks. Most of us begin a practice because of the benefits. Hard as it is, though, try to forget these in the moment and practice simply for its own sake. No grasping. Forget about the end result. Pay attention to how it feels to meditate in each passing second, and nothing more. As with exercise that ultimately becomes a more enjoyable experience when you're fully in the moment, relishing how your body feels as you stretch and work your muscles, so does meditation become totally gratifying when you surrender yourself to the experience.

If you are too impatient for quick results, you may be tempted to flit from one technique to another, confusing yourself and never giving any one method a chance to work. Experimentation is great, but be modest in your expectations. No meditation session, no matter what technique you use, can radically alter your life as a whole with a single go. Give a new routine a good few weeks before deciding it isn't for you.

Low self-esteem and doubt can be a particularly pernicious obstacle to meditation. You may overanalyze and wonder if you're doing it right, becoming self-conscious rather than self-aware! Appraising the meditation process as it happens actually just takes you out of the moment, and ultimately demotivates you.

To overcome this, remind yourself that it's OK to be on a learning curve. Just keep going—more familiarity and clarity will come with time. It's OK to be uncertain, or to make mistakes. Nobody is watching or judging you! Ask questions, keep learning, and don't worry about doing it perfectly. If you can bring your mind back after it wanders—then don't worry, you're doing it right.

Be kind to yourself and don't beat yourself up if you miss a session, or have a "bad" session. Self-criticism is only another distraction—mindfully and compassionately let it go.

Finally, there may be a bunch of things you routinely do outside of meditation that actually interfere with your attempts. Allowing your mind to spin out of control throughout the rest of the day is going to make meditation much harder. You can't undo a day's worth of binge-drinking and junk food with ten minutes at the gym, and you can't counteract a day of chaos and stress with a ten-minute mindfulness session, no matter how relaxing.

Is your life disorganized, erratic, or bursting with emotional volatility? Do you constantly fill your mind with noise—news, social media, movies, gaming, internet? Information overload can be so intense it takes an entire meditation session just to come down off the dopamine high. Do you engage in bad habits that undermine your overall health, like under-sleeping, never exercising, or drinking too much coffee?

Meditation is great, but it's not a magical mind vitamin that will cancel out a terrible daily diet of mindless information consumption and unhealthy habits. The more your non-meditating life is in alignment with your meditating one, the more results you'll see.

In this vein, let's briefly mention not just the quantity of information you're bombarding your nervous system with daily, but its *quality*. Unfortunately, much of the noise we encounter on social media, in the news and online, in TV and movies, and (perhaps worst of all) in advertising, is deliberately designed to capture our attention by force and hold it hostage.

Flashy, emotive and hard to look away from, these images and words affect us deeply, cognitively and emotionally, not to mention they actively instigate feelings of desire, craving, strong emotions, distraction, and addiction.

A little mindfulness in our media consumption can do wonders. Simply notice what you're feeding your brain, day in and day out. What effect is it really having to read that rage-inducing article online, to watch that depressing documentary, or to engage in the Instagram scrolling that leaves you feeling utterly worthless as a human being?

A "media detox" can help you calm down, recenter, and take charge of your own awareness again, not to mention boosting self-regulation and saving you a bunch of wasted time. Put mindful limits on what you consume, how, why, how often, and for how long. This may be as simple as deciding you will not start every day by reaching for your phone within seconds of waking up.

How to Address Meditation Challenges

If you're encountering constant mental chatter, remind yourself: it's not a problem. Thinking is what brains do. You're not trying to eliminate thoughts, just become aware of them, and in doing so, find space and distance. The trick is that resisting and avoiding is simply more of the same—so don't resist. Just notice.

This is what it really means to have an attitude of compassionate acceptance—to not cling to some idea of how you should be, but to simply welcome what is. Are you feeling restless and agitated? OK. That's how you are right now. Sit with that. Has a strong emotion emerged within you? OK. It's no less worthy of your kind attention than any other sensation.

When you stop resisting, you'll notice something interesting—things flow. It's the grasping or pushing against certain sensations that makes meditation feel difficult and conflict-ridden. When we let go, we see that there is no need to control or force or prevent or cultivate anything. The present moment is just right, exactly as it is.

And it changes! Anger, sadness, or restless legs don't seem like such a big deal when you notice that they are never permanent, but rise and fall in the moment, like waves, disappearing just as they arrived. Go deeper and watch how your consciousness itself is also moving and changing over time.

In the beginning, impediments to meditation may seem big and obvious, but they become more subtle the more you practice. You may notice yourself getting up after a session feeling slightly disappointed, perturbed by an unconscious desire to achieve …something. A state of bliss, a happy flash of insight or some deep calm as your reward for being so disciplined?

Again, these sensations are just waves in the ocean. In time, you may start to see that awareness is its own reward, that the present moment is sufficient in itself, and that all you can ever really do is be who you already are, in the ever-unfolding, perfectly formed, peaceful moment.

Making Meditation a Learned Habit

Researchers from the University College London have found that it takes around sixty-six days for a habit to become cemented or, as they put it, for a person to develop "automaticity." That said, there also seems to be large variation between individuals—some participants took as little as eighteen days while others took a whopping 254 days. Naturally, the kind of habit in question also determines how easy it is to adopt in the long term.

How long does it take for meditation to become a fixed habit? There's no telling. But committing to regular practice in the beginning is far more important than trying to tough out super-long sessions before you've properly established a habit.

To help your new meditation habit really stick, there are a few simple but powerful tricks you can use, for example "habit anchoring." Choose a thirty-second activity that will prompt you to meditate—like stretching, counting breaths or saying a mantra—and then connect this thirty seconds to an established habit you already have, such as getting out of the shower, waking up, or making your morning cup of coffee.

This way, you tack on a new habit to an old one by way of a smaller activity that will kick-start your momentum. For example, you always have your bedtime routine, but now you're reminding yourself to do a quick stretch beforehand, which leads you into a ten-minute loving-kindness meditation practice.

The "habit loop formula" is a related idea. A loop consists of a cue, a reward and a craving, and to establish a new routine (such as a morning meditation practice), you'll need all three.

A cue is something that triggers behavior, for example you waking up in the morning. A reward is a benefit for doing the behavior, such as feeling calm and centered after a morning meditation practice.

Finally, craving refers to the urge you feel when your brain *associates these two*—connecting the cue with the expected reward, i.e. when you wake up, your brain associates meditation with beneficial feelings of calm, which it then craves.

By deliberately strengthening the association of the cue and the feelings of reward, you anchor the behavior. Do this by mentally conjuring up the positive benefits of meditation every time you experience your cue, and thus cement in your mind the fact that you enjoy and crave meditation.

The process won't be automatic at first, but every time you follow through, you strengthen those loops and take one step closer to an automatic habit.

Make sure your environment supports your habit by giving yourself time and space and reducing clutter, and be clear and honest about your true motivations for taking up a meditation practice—you'll need to tap into this deep motivation on tired or lazy days when you don't feel like meditating! Choose a meditation style you actually like and hold yourself accountable. Give yourself a little reward once you complete each session or track your progress so you can see your self-discipline strengthening with time.

Most importantly, just keep going! Expect that it won't be easy to start a new daily habit, whatever it is. Don't be discouraged if you slip up; just get back into your routine as soon as you can. A skipped session or a difficult time isn't a sign that something is going wrong—but coming back to your practice no matter what is proof that you're strengthening your resolve, committing to your well-being and giving yourself the opportunity to really develop.

The Takeaway:

- Meditation is the deliberate and consistent cultivation of awareness, focus, and relaxation.
- Some widespread notions about meditation are nothing but myths. You don't need to convert to Buddhism or even incorporate religious elements in your practice. Meditation is not selfish avoidance of reality; rather, it cultivates full acceptance of reality. Meditation also does not require fighting with yourself just to keep your mind clear.
- While mindfulness is generally taken to be a state that can be fostered through the practice of meditation, some people consider mindfulness as itself a form of meditation, along with other forms such as yoga, tantra, and visualization.
- There are many different types of meditation, and you can practice the

one you resonate most with. Guided meditation involves a recorded voice or live teacher leading a structured meditation session. Loving-kindness meditation trains you to yield your conscious awareness toward developing self-compassion. Mantra meditation has you speak out a repeated or meaningless word or sound to anchor you in the present. In breathing meditation, you focus on your breath in order to stay in the moment. Mindfulness meditation involves a conscious practice of nonjudgment and non-attachment while cultivating awareness of the present.

- It's best to have a routine as to when and where you meditate. Choose a time and place where you're relatively free from distractions. Most important is that your practice is consistent and that you approach it with a willingness to meet each moment with calm, kind awareness.
- Among the most common challenges in meditation are lack of consistency,

expecting too much, impatience, low self-esteem and doubt, and an out-of-control, racing mind resulting from a highly stimulating day with a lot of stresses and unhealthy habits.

- It will take time to make meditation a habit, but you can help it along by attaching it to other daily habits you already have. Habit anchoring, a technique wherein you designate a thirty-second activity as a prompt for your meditation practice, helps you incorporate meditation more easily in your daily life. You can also employ the habit loop formula, which consists of a cue, a reward, and a craving as elements of establishing a new routine.

Chapter 4. How to Overcome and Defeat Everyday Eruptions

"Drink your tea slowly and reverently, as if it is the axis on which the whole earth revolves—slowly, evenly, without rushing toward the future; live the actual moment. Only this moment is life."

- *Thích Nhất Hạnh*

These days, meditation has become popular enough that no self-respecting lifestyle guru or wellness influencer would claim they do anything other than meditate daily. The aesthetic of mindfulness has infiltrated all aspects of life, and many people now consider some form of mindfulness a self-care basic like taking vitamins or going to the gym. *Of course* we all want to be calmer, kinder and more Zen in everyday life.

But fewer people will admit to finding meditation difficult, unappealing, or just challenging to squeeze into a modern busy life. You sit down to meditate with the best will in the world, but it's not so easy. What if you have a two-year old nagging at you to pay her attention, a stressful meeting in fifteen minutes, and a head simply bursting with items on your to-do list?

For the Busy Bee

In a way, we can practice meditation best when we are out in the "real world." Sitting serenely in a minimalist room with a water feature trickling in the corner is lovely, but not altogether feasible for most of us. We've already seen why it's worthwhile to start a more formal sitting meditation practice, but that's not the be all and end all of living a content, mindful life.

We can be mindful *all the time.* No matter how busy we are, where we find ourselves or the challenges we encounter, it can all become a part of our ongoing practice. As long as we are alive and there is a present moment to become aware of, we can be mindful. The idea is that mindfulness isn't over once your alarm rings and your ten-minute meditation is over for the day.

As you go about "normal life," remind yourself to breathe deeply. Simply doing this for a few seconds a dozen times throughout the day is like injecting a mini-meditation session right where you need it. Stop in the middle of writing that report, close your eyes, and take a few deep, luxurious breaths. Savor the air nourishing your body. Reconnect to the moment—it doesn't matter if you only have three seconds before the chaos of life beckons you again. Three seconds can be an infinity!

Even if you don't have a full half hour to complete a comprehensive mindfulness journaling session, grab a notepad and pen and doodle for five minutes as you empty your head. Put down all your thoughts in a "brain dump"—scribble it all down and tell yourself you can come back to it all later, if you really want to.

It doesn't matter what mundane activities you are in the middle of—you can do them all mindfully. Take time to really feel the fabric against your fingertips as you fold the laundry. Tidy your desk while you simultaneously clear away thought clutter in your mind. Notice the quality of the light on the steps as you walk across the courtyard to your next class, or sink into the task of putting letters into envelopes, turning it into a practice as profound and beautiful as a Japanese tea ceremony.

There's a famous Zen koan that goes, "Before enlightenment; chop wood, carry water. After enlightenment; chop wood, carry water."

This really is a wonderful way of saying that mindfulness doesn't magically transform the world around you. Being aware doesn't cast an otherworldly pink glow on everything, and spare you having to do "ordinary" life activities. Our perspective changes, but the outside is always as it is. In a deeper way, with awareness we more perfectly recognize the outside world for what it is, and come full circle—for the first time, we are able to delve into true reality. Chopping wood, carrying water, in all its natural, perfect, uncomplicated "is-ness." Nothing more, nothing less.

Maybe you feel like you can't meditate because you're busy. Well, meditate on the busyness. Try to do just one thing at a time—hint: it is actually impossible to do anything else! So you might as well pay attention right now; the next moment will come in its own time.

Slow down. Delegate some tasks if you can. Do less, and do what you do more mindfully. Have a tea or water break, stretch or take a few minutes to stare wistfully out of the window. Smell the wind. Wiggle your toes. As Thích Nhất Hạnh says, only this moment is life.

If you work at a job that doesn't exactly allow you to zone out throughout the day, don't worry—there's still plenty you can do to practice mindfulness during working hours. Remember, it's not so much the duration of a meditation practice that matters as its consistency. Finding just a few minutes to be mindful on a regular basis can leave you feeling refreshed, balanced, and able to tackle workplace stress and demands.

Use what you have. If you drive to and from work, use your commute as a meditation bell or habit anchor. For example, stop for two minutes every time you get in or out of your car to still your mind and gather your awareness. It may sound silly, but even a bathroom break can be the perfect opportunity for a mindfulness practice. Splash some cool water on your face, and spend a moment or two in a quiet stall to find your breath or perhaps say a quick mantra.

If you're at a desk, pick an interesting object to quietly focus on for a few moments. Look at it closely, examine its texture and weight, and bring your mind back to it if it wanders, in the same way as you would return to your breath in a mindfulness meditation. This is a quick, unobtrusive way to reconnect to the present without interfering with your workday—in fact, it's likely to make you *more* focused and calm.

If you like, try using headphones that play white noise, binaural beats, relaxing nature sounds or something similar, to help you get into a relaxed and focused state as you work. If you truly are busy, then your work itself can become a meditation practice. Focus entirely on it, gently calling your attention back when it wanders. Take note of your posture, your breath, and your thoughts as you work.

Don't rush. During your lunch break, you might be able to take a walk—make it a walking mediation by focusing on what you can see, hear, and smell. Jot down some notes in a journal or simply take the chance to fill your lungs with fresh clean air. When you're in a meeting, slow down and speak mindfully, really paying attention to what colleagues are saying, or trying to bring a little compassion and acceptance into the proceedings.

For the Perpetually Dissatisfied

Is mindfulness and meditation a way of life, a special practice, or a therapeutic technique to help with some particular problem? Actually, it can be all three.

We can try to cultivate a general sense of mindfulness as we go about our daily lives, but we can also dedicate some time to practicing a more formal sitting meditation routine. Finally, we can use the principles of mindfulness in a more acute way, as a stress-management technique.

Mindfulness can be a real solution to a hyper-stressful society. Mindfulness-based stress reduction is now studied in universities all over the world as a practical method for stress management. Furthermore, by using any of the approaches outlined in previous chapters, you give yourself the chance to avoid activating the stress response in the first place.

Mindfulness can teach you to take your thoughts a little less seriously, and switch from a hectic "doing" mode to a simpler "being" mode. By reining in your reactivity, you create space to respond more moderately, taking into account how your body feels rather than remaining entirely in your head. With compassion and acceptance, your entire attitude toward stress and adversity changes—you are less likely to respond with judgment and panic and more likely to be compassionate with yourself and others, and find calm, focused solutions to problems.

Many of us can diligently stick to a meditation practice when times are OK, but find it enormously challenging to remain consciously aware during times of crisis. Luckily, you can use meditation as a more deliberate response to stressful situations.

Start as you would any other meditation session, i.e. get comfortable, find your breath and posture, and get into a calm and relaxed state of mind.

Take your time to flesh this stressful situation out in your mind's eye. Imagine it vividly, immersing yourself in the picture. Notice where the stress expresses itself on your body—do you feel tight across your shoulders, or tension in your jawline? Breathe into this and stay with it for a moment.

Next, notice your emotional state. Use kind and accepting attention to really inhabit your feelings. You may even place a hand on the location on your body where you feel pain or discomfort, as though you were comforting a friend or a scared child.

Remember that you are not there to fix anything. You are not trying to soothe out a rough patch, or convince yourself not to feel how you feel, or draw a curtain over the experience and forget about it. All you are doing is being with the stressful sensation, without judgment, without looking to the next moment, without looking for ways to deny or avoid.

This technique may seem counterintuitive to those who are chronically stressed—doesn't sitting with stress simply make you more anxious?

The trick is that you are not ruminating any further, or engaging in any planning, strategizing, interpreting, judging, solving, or appraising. You are just there to *be*. There's no need to devise a story about what you're experiencing and why, or to push or pull against it. You are not explicitly trying to calm yourself down, but feeling calmer is a typical side effect of this practice. What you are primarily doing is **meeting your stressful experience head-on, in the moment, with nothing but kind attention.**

Nevertheless, there are countless relaxation techniques that can be used to actively soothe and calm a stressed-out mind, and these can be employed in conjunction with a mindfulness-based practice. Deep breathing is one such technique that can powerfully release stress in the body, and can be combined with almost every other stress-management activity.

One breathing technique is called square breathing. Lie on the floor with one hand on your chest and one on your belly. Breathe in through your nose and into your stomach, feeling it rise as you count slowly from one to four. Try to move the hand on your chest as little as possible, while breathing deeply and fully into your belly. Hold the breath for another four counts, then breathe out. As you breathe out, ease the air slowly out through your mouth for another four counts. You may purse your lips to help slow down your exhalation.

Not only does belly breathing fill your body with oxygen, slow your heart rate and decrease your blood pressure, it also stimulates the vagus nerve, which instigates a relaxation response across your entire body and makes you feel calmer.

Deep breathing exercises work to ease tension and chaos in your mind as the slow, steady breaths are incompatible with the quick, shallow breaths typical of the stress response. So instead of your mental and emotional state dictating how your body reacts, you can reverse the process and have your body—through slow, deep breaths—influence your mind to be serene and composed.

A "body scan" is another wonderful stress management and relaxation technique that can be used with or without meditation and mindfulness. Again, the body is an anchor into the present moment, and a point of focus to bring back a wandering mind.

Lie down somewhere comfortable where you won't be disturbed for a while, uncross your arms and legs, and close your eyes. Take a few moments to slow down and focus on your breath for a moment. Then, as though your consciousness were like a spotlight, shine your awareness on different parts of your body, one at a time.

Start at your feet. Focus on nothing but the sensation of having your feet—what can you feel?

With awareness, you might notice you can actually sense the skin across the surface of your foot, the weight of your heel pressing into the floor, or the soft fabric of your socks against your toes. You can focus on each toe individually, starting from one side and moving through all ten toes, spending a good few seconds on each one, just checking in with it, and observing how it feels.

As you notice sensations, let go of any judgments about what is good or bad, or what certain sensations mean. If you find you are tense somewhere, you don't need to immediately jump in and relax those muscles—just become aware. After a moment, you might like to breathe more deeply into the feeling, whatever it is, and notice if more relaxation arises.

Then move on to the soles of your feet and then heels, lavishing complete attention on each part, without rushing. Move on to your ankles, then slowly up your body, to your calves, knees, thighs, hips, belly, and so on until you are focusing on your chin, eyes, forehead, even your scalp. Of course, the body is all one piece, so it's up to you which parts you decide to zero in on and how long you linger.

If you encounter pain, discomfort, an itch, or a strange sensation, linger a little longer there. Breathe deeply and imagine the breath flowing through your body, moving to the area, bringing space and awareness so it can just be what it is. Notice any areas where you feel extra sensitive and inflamed, as well as places you feel numb. In scanning your body, you are simply trying to see where and how you are. Fully inhabit the sensations you encounter, without pushing against them.

A body scan is an excellent way to start or end a more formal meditative practice, and is also a great standalone relaxation technique at bedtime or during stressful periods. It's a technique that can encourage body-mind connection and can alert you to the tiny physiological events and sensations that would otherwise be missed by a busy mind.

Some people like to combine a body scan with elements of visualization—i.e. the practice of using your mind's eye to imagine a scene or imagery, usually for relaxation purposes. In traditional meditation, images are not deliberately conjured up; rather, the mind's activities are observed without attachment. But with visualization, you deliberately give your mind a soothing image or scene to focus on.

Essentially, you begin as you would any other meditation practice—sit or lie quietly somewhere and focus for a moment on the breath. Eyes closed, try to conjure up an image of something restful or calming, like a serene beach, a beautiful fantasy landscape, a cozy room with gentle rain outside and crackling fire in the corner, or an ancient temple strewn with petals.

Take your time to really flesh out this place—the sights, sounds, smells, tastes, and even feelings it evokes. Imagine even the tiniest details and textures. You may find it easier at first to do a guided meditation where the scene is described to you and you are prompted to explore it, or you can make your own recording to personalize your guided visualization. You may like to add appropriate white noise or nature sounds to complete the experience, although this isn't necessary.

Engage all your senses, and let your busy mind still for a moment. Forget about worries and rumination. In your visualization, you can do what you want—picture a ball of radiant gold light that you step into to feel safe and happy, or bathe in a magical fountain that washes away stress. Imagine yourself standing in a hazy glade of enormous trees, grass between your toes, as the wind blows over every part of you, taking your anxieties away with it. It's up to you!

If these relaxation techniques sound a little too time-consuming, don't worry, they needn't be. You can experience effective stress relief and relaxation in just a few minutes. Try a quick three-minute breathing practice: begin in the first minute by asking, "How am I right now?" Spend a minute checking in with your thoughts and feelings, and put a name to the sensations or emotions you're experiencing.

In the next minute, sink deeper into simply being aware of your breath. If thoughts and feelings emerge, gently let them go and return to the breath, in and out. For the final minute, go into your body—

spread awareness out over your physical experience in the moment.

This may seem like a simple and straightforward practice, but it very quickly teaches you to pause, become aware of your mental and emotional state, and then ground down into the present reality, as it's felt in your breath and your body. Within three minutes you can quickly reorient yourself, let go of stress and give yourself a window in the day to really remember who you are, and what you're doing.

Finally, no discussion of relaxation techniques is complete without considering stretching. Bearing in mind what we know about making certain behaviors automatic habits, consider adding on a relaxing stretching practice to the beginning or end of your normal exercise routine. Not only will you avoid rushing into physical activity and risking injury, but you'll give yourself a chance to really check in, be present, and notice how you're actually doing in the moment.

Stretching improves flexibility and boosts circulation—not to mention it just feels good! Although yoga certainly has benefits, you don't have to do a full yoga practice. Stretching is an intuitive human activity we all know how to do. Nevertheless, take care not to stretch to the point of pain, and go slowly and gently.

Try this: take a few deep breaths before you start, then move into the stretch until you feel that familiar pull—not pain. Now, still in position, relax the muscle as much as possible. Then, tighten or tense it again, still in position, before fully relaxing it once more. From here, you can stretch a little further than your previous limit. You can repeat the process as often as you like, but make sure you're going slowly and breathing deeply throughout.

When you stretch, stay mindful, and be present with how it feels. Notice any asymmetries in your body, tight or sore spots, or places where you can feel the effects of a workout. It makes a lot of sense to combine stretching, relaxation techniques, meditation, and daily exercise.

You can establish a daily flow and routine that gets you moving but also more relaxed and mindful, ready to return to the rest of your day feeling refreshed and calm.

Tips for effective stress management in a busy world

Be comfortable. There's no reason you can't try to be mindful at your desk or practice a three-minute body scan at work, but as far as you can, try to make sure you're always in a relaxed and comfortable position where you won't be distracted.

If your mind wanders, it's OK. Go easy on yourself—the goal is not to beat yourself up if you're not as mindful as you like. If you notice you're getting carried away in your head again, simply return to the breath. Watch where it goes, in detail. Feel it entering your nostrils, notice the rise and fall of your chest, the slight temperature difference between inhale and exhale…

Call out rumination and mind-wandering when it happens—i.e., say to yourself "thinking" or "planning" as you notice yourself doing these things, and perhaps spare a moment of joyful gratitude for your consciousness coming back.

Don't worry if you can only manage a few minutes here, a few minutes there. Consistency and frequency are more important than squeezing in a lengthy session. Remember—it's OK to experience distractions or a wandering mind. You are not trying to eliminate any of this, just become aware of it.

The Takeaway:

- The practice of meditation and mindfulness does not need to be confined within a ten-minute session in a completely silent room—these techniques can be employed even during regular activities you do in your daily life.
- Whether you're writing a report, folding laundry, or tidying your desk, you can endeavor to engage in mindfulness. No matter who you

are, how busy your life is or what challenges you are facing, you can always practice meditation and mindfulness. With effort and creativity, you can find ways to meditate at work, during errands or around the house.
- Practicing meditation does not mean that you can do away with life's humdrum routines after you've achieved heightened consciousness. Rather, meditating while you perform daily tasks will lead you to a deeper connection and genuine engagement with the present reality, along with its every routine chore and activity.
- Principles of mindfulness are especially useful when applied to reduce stress in the midst of life's hustle and bustle. Mindfulness-based stress reduction techniques help you break free of a hectic "doing" mode to a more tranquil yet purposeful "being" mode.
- A basic yet powerful technique in mindfulness practice is deep

breathing. It involves breathing in through your nose and into your stomach, feeling your belly rise, and breathing out slowly through your mouth. This breathing exercise helps slow your heart rate, decrease your blood pressure, and relaxes your body.
- Body scan, another stress-reduction technique, entails focusing your awareness on different parts of your body, one at a time. As you notice every sensation, tension, and discomfort you are experiencing, your body serves as an anchor to bring you to full awareness of the here-and-now.
- Visualization, a relaxation practice wherein you conjure a scene or image of something peaceful or calming, also helps relieve stress by steering your mind away from negativity and immersing it instead in a soothing mental picture.
- Stretching, a technique you can perform in itself or incorporate in your exercise routine, not only

boosts your circulation and increases flexibility, but also helps calm the mind when done mindfully.
- With meditative habits ingrained in your everyday routine, you can meet every experience and sensation you have with kind attention instead of heavy drudgery.

Chapter 5. A Path to Fulfilment and Satisfaction

"With every breath, the old moment is lost; a new moment arrives. We exhale and we let go of the old moment. It is lost to us. In doing so, we let go of the person we used to be. We inhale and breathe in the moment that is becoming. In doing so, we welcome the person we are becoming. We repeat the process. This is meditation. This is renewal. This is life."

– Lama Surya Das

The more you practice meditation and cultivate mindful living, the easier and more natural it will become, and the more you'll notice the subtle yet profound changes it brings to every moment of your life. Learning to conduct yourself with eternal, quiet wonder of the present moment and a willingness to embrace it and yourself exactly as you find it—this is a gift in itself.

Used in this way, meditation is not a cure, not an escape and not some attempt to improve on an unwanted present moment. Nevertheless, the irony is that in learning to be still with and accept the present moment, we often *do* end up improving on it. If you've practiced meditation for long enough, and seen the results in your own life, you may have wondered at its potential to tackle deeper emotional and behavioral issues like addiction, depression or anxiety.

Gaining Awareness to Break Bad Habits and Enhance Self-Control

One thing meditation may help with is breaking bad habits.

What is a bad habit, when you really think about it? Just as the ground gets worn with ruts in the places people most often walk, our brains become imprinted with our most well-used neural pathways. Just as our muscles and organs get used to repeated actions until they become automatic, so do the neurons in our brains, eventually firing on autopilot without our conscious awareness.

The ability to form habits has been essential for our species' long-term survival. Having a reward-based feedback system ensures we gravitate toward behaviors that lead us to fulfillment. First, we learn by making associations between stimuli, e.g. drinking always accompanies enjoyable time spent with friends and pleasant conversation. We engrave in our minds memories of these associations, and in the future, learn to anticipate them—case in point, drinking in the expectation that it will lead to more of the same sociable, happy feelings.

In time, this behavior can establish a craving or urge in us, and we start to look to certain stimuli as a source of feeling good, solving problems, or avoiding pain. Maybe you start to reach for alcohol every time you feel alone or bored or unhappy, hoping that it will somehow fix the bad emotions or create good ones. So the next time you're in a problematic situation, maybe you drink again, taking concrete action to strengthen those old mental pathways. Maybe you do feel momentarily better, and the association is reinforced—you now have a particular relationship with drinking, held in place by triggers and cues that set you off down old familiar paths.

Alcohol, smoking and drugs are the first things that spring to mind when we think of addiction, but the truth is that most of us are probably far more addicted to the everyday, normal vices passively condoned by our society—caffeine, social media, junk food, sugar, gaming, even porn. Whenever each of these is consumed, our brains get a dopamine rush that fills us with feelings of pleasure, which in turn reinforces their continued consumption. Whenever we feel troubled, down, or even just bored, we crave the sensation of that dopamine hit again, making it harder and harder to stop the habit as we drive the addiction deeper and deeper in our system. Thus mediated by the dopamine reward channels in our brains, we get stuck in mental ruts, going round and round, even when our habits no longer bring us pleasure or even actively harm us.

This is where mindfulness can step in to help you get unstuck. When we're neck-deep into our cravings and addictions, we are reduced to mindlessness, as we lay down the power to recognize our own thoughts and instead gravitate only toward feeling good instantaneously. Mindfulness is the antidote to mindless, automatic habits, and helps us break long-entrenched cycles so we can lay down more consciously chosen, beneficial behaviors for ourselves. If you picture a bad habit as an endlessly reinforcing loop that goes round and round, then imagine mindfulness as a speed hump, or a little stopper that wedges into the cycle and gives you a chance to pause and make different choices.

Every bad habit is an attempt to actively avoid some kind of pain or seek some kind of pleasure—or else it was initially established for this reason and is now compulsively done on autopilot. A trigger for a bad habit is thus anything that cues us to act to relive pain or create pleasure. Often, once a bad habit is underway, we only need the faintest reminder to trigger us to engage in the bad habit again. We might have initially started overeating to get over a bad breakup, but carry on doing so just because we're triggered by a McDonalds ad on TV, a friend suggesting a meetup, a gap in the schedule, the clock striking noon or the slightest feeling of being hungry.

The trigger stimulates a response in us, physiologically, psychologically, or both. This feeling, whatever it is, can lead to sensations of craving. We may want the happy feeling to continue or the bad feeling to stop, but either way we feel the urge to behave a certain way—to overeat, for example.

Acting on the urge has an effect that we find beneficial and the behavior is reinforced, and thus the cycle repeats. Your addictive habit can be anything: shopping, smoking or drinking, self-criticism, mindless social media use, gaming or even love—if it's defined as the heady, obsessive early days of a new and uncertain romance.

Mindfulness, however, can put a spanner in the works at any point in this cycle.

In the beginning, when a stimulus presents itself, you can stop and become aware of its effect on you. In an addictive loop, you begin by appraising some sensations as either pleasant or unpleasant. Nut if you can face stimuli with calm and equanimity, you don't make this appraisal—you simply note the stimulus, without grasping or interpreting it either way. Notice the trigger and choose not to act, just be conscious of it.

You can also be mindful later on, when the urge to act arises. This compulsion is often invisible to you, and you scarcely think about it in the moment. There is often very little time between the compulsion to act and the action—but the fact remains that there is a gap between those two. Recognizing and taking a moment to just exist in this gap—neither being pushed by the compulsion nor being pulled by the anticipated satisfaction of the action—is the key to taking back your life from bad habits.

You can use mindfulness to realize the presence of that gap between the urge and the action, step in, pause and hold the possibility of *not* acting. This is a wonderful moment of clarity and calm, where we can see that going along with our habit is not the only option available to us.

Even if you don't remember to be mindful until after you've done the behavior, that's still OK. Notice how it feels to have closed the loop. If you're honest, you may become aware of a vague sense of unease, and the reward may seem a little shallower than you might have anticipated. Just be aware of this—it will loosen the positive associations you have with this behavior if you can clearly acknowledge that it's not all that satisfying anyway. Try not to beat yourself up for succumbing to temptation; just stay mindful of how the cycle is playing out in your body and mind.

Finally, it may not always be so easy to catch an addictive cycle or bad behavior in progress, especially in the case of older and more entrenched habits. Be patient with yourself. Consider two strings that have been knotted over and over again, in this way and that, throughout your childhood until adulthood. You wouldn't expect that long succession of knots to be untied in just a single sitting, right? The same is true with breaking free from a deeply entrenched bad habit. Much like how it takes multiple attempts along with a whole lot of patience and perseverance to untie years' worth of complicated knots, so does a bad habit need consistent practice of mindfulness (along with loads of patience and self-compassion) over a period of time to uproot it from your system.

We can have mindful awareness any other time, and gain awareness of how our behaviors are affecting us, what triggers them, how they are reinforced and how we can break the loops. When we develop more self-control outside of addictive behaviors, we can bring more mindfulness and self-awareness to the process as it unfolds, and as we are faced with a tempting trigger.

Even if you don't have a particularly serious addiction, you may still find enormous benefit in using mindfulness to target persistent cravings or distractions. The world is full of them, after all, and we could all use some help in reining in our attention and self-control when a bad habit threatens to shatter our self-discipline.

The following technique can be used any time you notice yourself being compulsively and maybe even addictively drawn to behave in a certain way. If you can have the presence of mind to wait out this urge, then a quick and targeted bout of meditation can help you dissipate it.

Your craving could be for an unhealthy snack, a cigarette, buying something online when you don't need it and can't afford it, and so on. It may be that you're compelled to act to make yourself feel better (e.g. zoning out in front of mindless TV because it makes you feel cheerful) or to avoid feeling bad (e.g. compulsively checking social media sites so you can avoid feelings of sadness and isolation).

If you've noticed the craving, well done. Take a moment now to find a comfortable position, and work through a quick cravings meditation. Begin by doing a body scan to check in with yourself and where you're at. Notice tension—addiction and craving usually comes with tightness in the gut, jawline, chest, neck and shoulders. You may also notice shallow breathing, a furrowed brow, racing thoughts, unsettled feelings in your stomach or even a watering mouth.

Sit with whatever it feels like to be in craving right now. Notice these living, fleeting sensations, and honor them by staying present without judging or resisting any of them. It can be enormously helpful to simply name the craving you're experiencing—speak its name and recognize that it's there. Notice the strange restlessness all over your body, for example, and greet it, saying its name "craving."

It might be a novel sensation in itself—the fact that **we can just sit with our cravings and observe them with curiosity and compassion, without necessarily giving in to them**. Notice what it feels like to pause and hold off on acting, i.e. to be in control of your cravings, rather than the other way around!

As you sit in quiet and alert acceptance, you may be surprised at what else comes up. Cravings can also be for subtler, more abstract things. Do you notice the temptation to escape into fantasies, or to get instantly caught up in a self-critical loop where everything you do is wrong? Hold it all in your compassionate, open awareness and simply let it be.

After around ten minutes, slowly and gently come out of your meditation and become aware of your surroundings again. Do a quick stretch and notice if you feel any different now compared to when you first sat down to meditate.

Even if you do end up succumbing to your bad habit, that's OK. Maintain awareness throughout, and notice if following through with the behavior is really all it's cracked up to be. Notice next time that holding out on temptation is not as hard as you might have thought, and that the world doesn't end just because you sit for a few minutes with an unpleasant sensation or craving.

With time, you might even see that the habit has very little to do with your overall well-being—i.e., you may realize that compulsive use of substances, food or distractions *doesn't* actually increase your well-being, self-esteem or overall happiness in life. By becoming aware of all this, you gradually start to unshackle yourself from the chains of habit and addiction.

How to Ease Emotional Turmoil

Humans are emotional beings. Each of us wants to be loved and accepted for who we are, and each of us is afraid of being forgotten, hurt, abandoned, or judged by others. For many people, emotions are swifter than any other experience, and rush to the fore well before any rational thought can argue otherwise. Even if we are intelligent, clear-minded individuals with plenty of self-discipline, we may be crippled by worry, self-doubt, anger, fear, sadness, deep shame, or full-blown panic at times.

Mindfulness can teach us to embrace all of these emotions, with serenity and peace. Learning to work with our emotions—especially the intense and unpleasant ones—can be challenging at times. But with an attitude of accepting presence, we can calm the rush of panic, soothe nervous systems jangled by anxiety, and heal old traumas that keep us stuck in doom and gloom.

We can use the process called "mindful inquiry" to help us work with difficult feelings. For many of us, this technique may be difficult because it is unlike many "positive thinking" or therapeutic approaches we may be used to. The difference is that we are not analyzing or interpreting anything, and not approaching ourselves like a troublesome puzzle to solve. We are also not trying to patch over uncomfortable feelings or cheer ourselves up.

Rather, with mindful inquiry, we are approaching our emotions with **courage, curiosity, and a willingness to observe and experience what is there.** This is deep exploratory work of your feeling self, and it requires you to both acknowledge and accept whatever it is you find when you plumb your emotional depths.

You don't have to approve of or condone a feeling to accept and acknowledge it. Just see it, and call it by its name, give it space to be what it is, without rushing to avoid it or get rid of it. You don't have to change a thing—just ride the wave you encounter, as you encounter it. If you struggle with panic and anxiety, bouts of depression or intense self-criticism and shame, try the following to bring some mindfulness to the experience.

As usual, begin seated comfortably in a quiet and undisturbed place. Turn off phones and devices. It's important you feel safe enough to sit with potentially strong emotions, so it's OK to hold off until you have a moment to yourself to give your emotions the attention they deserve. Take the time to breathe deeply, arrive at your practice and give a brief word of gratitude for finding the courage to do something good for yourself.

Spend a little while doing a body scan, and check in with yourself mentally, physically, and emotionally. *How are you?*

Breathe and open up, allowing yourself to become aware of your emotional state in the moment. There may be fresh feelings from events earlier in the day or old wounds and traumas that surface. Acknowledge every feeling and sensation as though you were welcoming each as a guest to a dinner table—every sensation has a place, no matter how intense or negative the experience they bring.

Now, without doing anything in particular about these emerging sensations, focus on your breath. Breathe naturally, and simply be alive here and now, one breath at a time. You could focus on just one part of your body as you still your mind and sit calmly with yourself in the quiet spaces between breaths. Focus on the tip of your nose, your belly button or chest rising and falling.

Once you are comfortably anchored in your breath and in your body, begin a mindful inquiry of the contents of your heart, body, and soul. The idea is that with gentle awareness, you can slowly become aware of whatever is beneath your ordinary perception that is driving your current state of panic, anger, fear, etc.

You are seeking understanding and insight, primarily by exploring and sinking into the bodily expression of your emotions. "Feel into" your emotional state—acknowledge all the emotions and sensations that arise in you, without excuse, analysis, judgment, appraisal or even approval. You may find that the more you sink into and really experience these feelings, the more they open up, and reveal a multitude of other thoughts and feelings within them.

You may discover that what you thought was one emotion is actually another. You may find that a long-standing core belief in your own worthlessness is being fueled by some painful memories from the past you largely ignore now, or some associations that you developed in childhood. Consider a child who only gets attention and affection from his parents whenever he receives a medal or is highly commended by teachers in school. He comes to associate acceptance and love with achievement, and believes he is worthless if he does not get recognition or praise from others. As an adult, he throws his back out still trying to garner praise and awards, and becomes exceedingly self-castigating when he fails. Unless he becomes mindful and cultivates awareness of the roots of these behaviors, he will continue to live in emotional turmoil.

By gently acknowledging what has remained out of awareness, you integrate these emotions and, ironically, give yourself a chance to let them go. After all, you would not be able to truly let go of something you weren't aware you held in the first place.

An insight occurs: it's the *resistance* to "bad" emotions that feels the worst, but, ironically, accepting and embracing them diminishes them somehow. Like weather or waves, our emotions can be felt as transitory and completely part of our experience, something we are more than capable of enduring and holding, then releasing again.

As you emerge from this meditation, wiggle your fingers, slowly open your eyes and come back to the present. What do you notice? You may discover a feeling of compassion and understanding for yourself. In turning toward even those difficult experiences and parts of ourselves, we may feel calmer and more whole.

It's this calm feeling that, incidentally, can make mindfulness meditation useful for dealing with insomnia. Going off to sleep with a clam, peaceful heart undoubtedly leads to better-quality sleep, too. A before-sleep meditation works because it takes us out of the striving mind, which anxiously tells us we *should* have fallen asleep already—and leads us further down the spiral of negative thoughts.

You can do a mindfulness practice of the type we've outlined already, and combine it with stretching before bed or a body scan once you've settled and are calm and tuned in to your breath. Gently bring your awareness to each part of your body and deliberately breathe into it, inviting deeper and deeper relaxation.

If your mind wanders and your head fills with thoughts, just tell yourself you can pick them up tomorrow if you really want to—right now, your only job is to take your time breathing, and feeling your body release and relax. Let the thoughts go.

You could count or try a mantra, but it's not strictly necessary. If you don't end up falling asleep, that's OK. Notice it all with the same kind awareness as always. Remind yourself that it's not the end of the world if you don't fall asleep—your body will still derive the benefits of the rest you're giving it, and being unhappy that you're not falling asleep will not make you drift off any faster anyway!

Mindfulness: Kindness, and Compassion, and Emotional Intelligence

In the beginning, mindful meditation seems rather simple—you sit alone quietly somewhere and mind your own business, calming your own thoughts and being a little kinder to yourself. Maybe you relieve your stress or feel better about yourself, or end up being a little more productive. But as you actually practice more and more, you will start to see that the benefits of this kind of practice extend far, far beyond your individual experience.

This is because there's a very fine line between non-judgmental, total acceptance and *compassion*.

What's more, compassion is something that's hard to isolate; if you have it for yourself, it's impossible not to extend it toward others, and to bring a little of that kindness to everything you do. Rather than it being some self-involved, private practice you do on your own time, meditation starts to look like a way of benefitting not just yourself, but everyone around you.

If compassion is thus so beneficial, why do we often find it in short measure? Why do some of us lack compassion, both for ourselves and for others? One factor may be adverse childhood experiences that have undermined our ability to regulate our own emotions and have empathy as well as trust in others. Growing up in a neglectful or abusive home, for instance, can potentially breed mistrust and a tendency to look after only one's own needs and safety, as a way to survive. Another factor may be our dog-eat-dog culture that encourages competition and judgment over an attitude of giving, helping, and understanding. When only one person can be "number one," people want to help only themselves and may even wish for the misfortune of others that they may more easily rise to the top.

Mindfulness can be seen as a way of updating these old modes of being—as though we were installing new and superior software onto the hardware that is our brain. The human operating system entails our psychological, emotional, behavioral and even spiritual tendencies—everything that mindfulness and meditation works to bring out into conscious awareness.

With mindfulness, we become aware of old programs that simply don't work for us anymore, and give ourselves the freedom to choose something better.

This state of healthy inner balance and self-awareness has been called emotional intelligence, EQ, and can be honed with, you guessed it, mindfulness practice. When we have high EQ, we are able to (among other things):

- Be aware of and identify our own emotions and sensations
- Take conscious responsibility for that experience
- Be compassionate and kind with ourselves and others
- Develop the ability to tolerate difficult emotions without resistance, i.e. low reactivity
- Keep distance from emotions and retain perspective
- Have healthy and beneficial interpersonal relationships with others

By now, it should be obvious that these competencies are precisely those honed by mindfulness practice. Whenever we meditate, we enhance our EQ, and this has a knock-on effect on every area of life where we have to encounter others—i.e. all of them. By adopting a mindful, compassionate, and serene approach to ourselves, we practice how to carry this attitude to others.

Mindfulness and compassion are not really as distinct as they first appear. And as we learn to love and accept what arises within *our own* hearts, minds and bodies, we learn how to turn that awareness to the outside, too, and feel compassion, awareness and acceptance for what we encounter *in others*. As we come to see ourselves in a more positive light, we also learn to view others in a more affirmative way. As Goethe put it, "A man sees in the world what he carries in his heart."

As we strengthen our own sense of well-being and self-esteem, we are more tolerant of other people's faults; as we learn to bring awareness to the present, we realize we are suddenly able to inhabit that space with others, too.

In meditation, we are neutral and unattached. But, curiously, a serene and stable mind seems to *want* to be compassionate and generous, to reach out in love and gratitude. Sadly, research conducted by University of Michigan's

Sarah Konrath suggests that people's concern for the welfare of others has been nosediving for the last thirty years, with self-reported compassion and empathy being extremely low, and dropping. People have moved away from a tribal way of living where each person takes pride in and is valued for what they can contribute to the group, and are increasingly moving toward an individualistic culture where each takes as much as they can, either for fear of running out of resources or due to a need to be superior to the rest. With this trend afoot, it is no doubt compassion for others has been pushed aside and division reigns over unification.

Can meditation and mindfulness help remedy this situation?

If we return to meditation's earliest history, we can see that many of the original proponents of mindfulness considered things like improved mood, memory and physical health as *side effects*—the main objective, from a less secular point of view, was nothing less than total enlightenment.

Being a matter of the soul or the essence of being itself, enlightenment was the realization of the oneness of all life, of the fleeting and illusory nature of suffering, of the dissolution of the ego, of the interconnectedness of life. Mindfulness and meditation, with their potential to lead to enlightenment, are thus antidotes to the selfish, dog-eat-dog culture that thrives in society nowadays. The more we recognize how all life is interconnected, the more we will care to look after others in the same way that we take care of ourselves.

In the more religious or spiritual framework, to meditate is to encounter the divine—the living, breathing, endless moment—and to experience the bliss of that perfect encounter. In this way, it would be hard to imagine how you could meditate and *not* cultivate profound feelings of compassion and beneficence.

Research has illuminated the mental, cognitive, and neuroanatomical changes that meditation brings, and its effects on stress management or productivity at work. However, relatively little research has been done on how meditation opens the heart and invites us to connect with others in a more authentic, empathetic way.

A Northeastern University research group led by Paul Condon has recently found that those who had attended an eight-week meditation course were three times more likely to offer their seat to a person on crutches than those who had not been part of such a course. It's an encouraging result—can we imagine a world where people are all kinder and more considerate of one another simply because they do a little meditation?

On the other hand, it's easy to imagine that a kind-hearted person could quickly become overwhelmed with the sheer amount of suffering in the world. Won't being more open and empathetic lead to compassion fatigue and apathy?

Luckily, mindfulness has an answer: research by Buddhist monk Matthieu Ricard and neuroscientist Tania Singer has shown that mindfulness training actually limits the activation of those neural pathways associated with witnessing others in distress, while strengthening pathways associated with social affiliation. This means, roughly, that we are able to feel and act with compassion, without delving into debilitating shared pain.

This bears a closer look—contrary to popular belief, we may best adapt to a harsh and unfair world filled with suffering not by hardening ourselves, but by cultivating compassion. The most profound benefit may not even be for us personally, but on a larger scale, as a question of compassion between families, communities, and nations.

It's hard to imagine what mindfulness couldn't improve, from foreign policy and government to domestic violence, interpersonal relationships, parenting, education, workplace conflict, therapy, crime rehabilitation, business, and healthcare.

We already briefly considered loving-kindness meditation in an earlier section, but let's take a closer look at this method, and how we can use this approach to increase our own emotional intelligence and compassion for self and others. Loving kindness isn't some difficult, abstract concept—we all know what it is because we've felt it before, those warm feelings of love, goodwill, acceptance, and appreciation for others.

Crucially, the attitude of loving kindness is not something that others have to earn from us by behaving in certain ways, and it's not something that we can only hope to achieve "one day" when we're super tolerant, enlightened people. Rather, compassion is something we can cultivate right now, and it doesn't mean we indiscriminately approve of everything and everyone, either. It's simple understanding for other people and what they are, without judgment.

The trick is that judgment comes from our thoughts. Compassion is actually quite a natural and easy state, only one that can be quickly overshadowed by mental chatter that invites us to compare, judge, appraise, criticize, cling to or reject what we see in others.

It's a symmetrical process—when we are familiar and understanding with our own pain, our own weaknesses and our own difficulties, we are so much better able to acknowledge and accept the same attributes when we find them in others.

We see that they are just like us—that they have fears and hopes, that they want to be loved, that they have been hurt and in many ways, they are just trying their best. We learn to love and accept ourselves and others as human beings who have intrinsic worth, no matter what experience we have in each passing moment.

The insight is this: that the essence inside all of us IS kindness and compassion, and we can see that more clearly when we quiet the endless ego-chatter of the mind.

Don't make the mistake of thinking that you can be kind to others all the while being self-critical or ashamed of who you are. We can only encounter others with the same spirit with which we approach ourselves. With compassion, there is no competition—the happiness of others is our happiness—

and there is no hierarchy, because compassion serves everyone involved in equal measure.

Self-healing becomes healing your connection with others.

Self-acceptance becomes acceptance of others and the journeys they are on.

Tolerating difficult emotions in ourselves makes us less reactive, hostile, or fearful of conflict or difference between us and others.

So, how do we begin?

How to Best Practice Loving-Kindness Meditation

Compared to other forms of meditation, loving kindness may seem a lot more straightforward and intuitive. It can be done anywhere and is flexible enough to be adapted as needed. There's also no real way to do it "wrong"—the end goal is to foster feelings of compassion and kindness, and as long as we turn up to our practice with this intention, we will be strengthening our own powers of empathy.

Loving kindness is for everybody, but may be particularly helpful if you're working through old resentments, trauma, or difficult experiences in the past. We could all use a little more love and compassion in our lives, whether we're dealing with self-hate and shame, a bad breakup, abuse, loneliness or feelings of anger and alienation, or simply want to become a nicer person to be around!

As with all other meditative practices, stay consistent. Start off your session by finding your breath, getting comfortable and sinking into the moment. Do a body scan if you like and relax your limbs into whatever position you've chosen. Set a timer for anywhere from two to fifteen minutes, or longer if you like.

Now, you are going to hold in your mind a kind of "blessing" or good wish, for example the phrase, "may you be well" or "may you be at peace." These are not just words, though—actively conjure up the *feeling* behind the phrase, a sense of warmth, acceptance, and benevolence. You could use visualization to picture warm, glowing pink light, smiling faces, a flowing river of love that connects everyone, or rays of light shooting out from your heart.

Start by invoking in your mind's eye somebody that you really love and care about. See their face in your imagination, and dwell on images of them laughing and smiling, being who they are. Allow yourself to feel warm love toward them—concentrate on this feeling, on how effortless and generous it is. You may notice that you can sustain this emotion even when thinking of bad things this person might have done to you, or their less than ideal qualities.

Next, conjure up the image of someone you like but don't necessarily love. See them in the same way, as a human being, doing their best, with good and bad qualities. Say your mantra ("May you be well") and try to cultivate a feeling of compassion toward them. Visualize yourself embracing them with a warm pink glow, or giving them a gift.

Carry on, imagining next a person who is an acquaintance. Can you see how this person, even though you don't know them well, is also someone's dearly beloved? How they are struggling with all the same challenges you are, how they crave love too? Say your mantra with their face in your mind's eye and revel in feeling compassion for them. Remember, you don't have to condone what they do or think they're perfect—just have compassion and understanding for who they are, exactly as they are.

Next, picture a total stranger, and do the same thing. Following that, imagine someone you actively dislike. This can be harder, but try anyway. If you feel resistant, give yourself some compassion and allow the situation to be what it is. Recognize your shared humanity. You may want to forgive, you may not; what matters is that you're deliberately opening your heart.

If you want to, you can consider extending this practice to include those people you feel you hate; those people who have hurt you the most. This is where loving-kindness meditation can be its most powerful. Use your mantra and send these people love, even though you also may have other feelings toward them. See them living a full life, with good and bad. Stand aside from it and let it all be.

Finally, you can turn your mantra and your warm light of compassion onto what may be the hardest person of all—yourself. For some people, starting with themselves is the easiest, and they begin with kindness to themselves before considering others. For others, they can more easily manage compassion for their enemies than they can for themselves! Simply notice it all, and hold it with kindness.

To finish your meditation, imagine all the world, with you and everyone in it, living their lives, being themselves, good and bad. See the whole human race, and everyone in the past and the future. See if you can imagine your heart being so immense it can expand to encompass everyone, including every non-human being, every animal and plant, *everything*. Look at it all with grace, benevolence, compassion, and empathy. See how everything is just fine. Just as it is, in all its complexity. Completely worthy of love.

You can add a journaling and contemplative element onto the end of this practice, to help you notice how the meditation makes you feel and whether there are any tangible changes in your perspective the more you practice. Are you finding it easier to hold kindness for certain people? Even if you can't do a full-on loving-kindness meditation as often as you'd like, try to recall that loving state of awareness by using mantras or phrases that resonate with you, such as:

May all beings be at peace

May you be safe, healthy and well

May there be love, forgiveness, understanding, and compassion

May I give and receive appreciation today

You can evoke feelings of loving kindness for a few moments before you have a meeting or conversation, or just before you type up an email. Do it before a date or interview, or after an argument to help you gain perspective and calm down before deciding how to respond. You may find that regularly doing loving-kindness meditation makes it so much easier to summon up those same feelings of sympathy throughout your day.

The Takeaway:

- Done consistently, there is no area of life that meditation and mindfulness cannot improve. The more you immerse yourself in the practice of mindfulness, the more you'll experience the gloriousness of every moment you find yourself in, whether it's simply carrying out a common chore or facing an unprecedented challenge.
- Bad habits and addictions often emerge from a need to experience pleasure or avoid pain. Because of the benefits they offer you in the immediate moment, these activities get imprinted in your brain through repeated reinforcement. Over time, they become automatic, mindless crutches during your weak moments.

- Mindfulness is an antidote against a mindless succumbing to the pull of bad habits. Cultivating mindfulness can help you break bad habits and manage your cravings by improving your self-control and bringing awareness and self-compassion to addiction cycles.
- Using mindfulness, you can disrupt bad habits at several points during their cycle. Right at the start, meet tempting triggers with calmness and equanimity. When you feel the urge to act, use mindfulness to notice the gap between impulse and action, and realize that engaging in the bad habit is not the only option. Even if you've already done the bad action, you can still employ mindfulness as you become aware that the rewards of such behavior are not as satisfying as you had anticipated after all.
- Mindfulness can improve self-control, help you manage cravings, break bad habits and bring

awareness and compassion to addiction cycles.
- Mindfulness can help you better self-regulate through strong emotions such as fear and anger, by using mindful inquiry to gently tap into the deeper roots of our experience. Mindful inquiry has you resist from interpreting or analyzing anything, and instead leads you to approach your emotions with curiosity and an unconditional openness to simply observe and fully experience what is.
- Through mindfulness, we gain awareness of old patterns and tendencies we have acquired in our childhood or environment which do not work for us anymore, and we empower ourselves to choose actions and build habits that benefit us instead.
- Loving-kindness meditation can foster love and compassion for ourselves and others, which helps improve our emotional intelligence and interpersonal relationships.

Summary

CHAPTER 1. THE ART OF BEING PRESENT

- Mindfulness is a quality of consciousness—the state of being aware of your experience in the present moment, without judgment.
- Mindfulness is not a fixed trait but an **attitude** that anyone can cultivate.
- While mindfulness and meditation are related concepts, they are not one and the same. Mindfulness is a state, while meditation is an activity. Through meditation, one can achieve a state of mindfulness.
- Mindfulness can help with all aspects of life, as it is not a specialized condition and is instead a state of awareness you can harness in each passing moment of your lived experience.

- Research has shed light on the numerous benefits of mindfulness. When engaged in consistently, mindfulness brings about an increased sense of calm, greater concentration and focus, reduced stress levels, improved mood, better memory, and enhanced emotional regulation.
- Much of the modern secular philosophy of mindfulness has its roots in ancient Hindu and Buddhist tradition. Putting emphasis on cultivating awareness and acceptance as well as incorporating meditation in their rituals, both religions have the concept of mindfulness central to their practice.
- In the modern era, mindfulness has been a buzzword in positive psychology and self-help arenas, taking on a variety of forms including as a self-care technique, as a way to improve employee well-being, and as a tool for coping with stress, adversity, and emotional struggles.

- Neuroscience has pointed out that the brain has two separate neural networks: the "narrative circuit" which constantly tells stories and interprets our experiences, and the "direct experience circuit" which processes the present moment through our sensory organs. One of mindfulness's benefits is to help us switch from the "narrative circuit" to the "direct experience circuit" so that we can achieve a heightened sense of awareness and calm in our daily life.
- The seven basic pillars of mindful living, as put forward by Joe Kabat-Zinn, are (1) an attitude of non-judgment and non-attachment, (2) beginner's mind, (3) patience, (4) trust, (5) acceptance, (6) non-striving, and (7) release into the flow.
- Note that some conceptual and research limitations exist as to the study of mindfulness's effects, so it's best to approach this practice slowly and with modest expectations—that is, take care to explore mindfulness mindfully.

Chapter 2. Everyday Mindfulness for Mental Calm

- Meditation is not the same as mindfulness, which can be practiced right now, no matter what you are doing. Each day presents opportunities to enter a state of heightened awareness, in the ordinary activities that you engage in—from washing your face, to eating, to the daily commute, to your interactions with others.
- A common myth about the practice of mindfulness is that it requires total emptiness of the mind, where every emerging thought is blocked by a wall to prevent it from disturbing a pure, flawless Zen state. In reality, however, the mind **will** wander—and you are not required to completely stop it from doing so.
- In mindfulness, you can allow your mind to wander, and work instead toward simply becoming aware,

notice the stream of thoughts without becoming attached to it, and anchor back to the now. All you need is an attitude of non-striving, acceptance, patience, and the willingness to consistently and gently bring yourself back to the present.

- A way to come back to the present moment is to tune in to your breathing. As the breath remains constant no matter what time of the day it is or what activity you engage in, breathing is a natural anchor you can use to bring yourself back to the now. Focusing on how your breath moves in and out of you leads you to redirect your consciousness to what is in the here and now.
- In addition to breathing, your body's sense perceptions (from your eyes, ears, nose, tongue, and skin) are effective anchors you can employ to activate your direct experience circuit instead of your narrative circuit.
- You can be mindful when you interact with others. As you talk with

the person in front of you, really see them, be fully with them, and immerse yourself in their world for the time that you are with them.
- Practice mindfulness as you read, write, and listen. Mindful reading allows a space for absorption, reflection, and insight to boom. Mindful writing sharpens your capacity for keen observation, discernment, and faithful documentation of what is. Mindful listening grants you the ability to remain calm, open, and accepting of the other person's being as an expression of the present moment.

CHAPTER 3. MELDING MINDFULNESS WITH MEDITATION

- Meditation is the deliberate and consistent cultivation of awareness, focus, and relaxation.
- Some widespread notions about meditation are nothing but myths. You don't need to convert to Buddhism or even incorporate religious elements in your practice.

Meditation is not selfish avoidance of reality; rather, it cultivates full acceptance of reality. Meditation also does not require fighting with yourself just to keep your mind clear.

- While mindfulness is generally taken to be a state that can be fostered through the practice of meditation, some people consider mindfulness as itself a form of meditation, along with other forms such as yoga, tantra, and visualization.
- There are many different types of meditation, and you can practice the one you resonate most with. Guided meditation involves a recorded voice or live teacher leading a structured meditation session. Loving-kindness meditation trains you to yield your conscious awareness toward developing self-compassion. Mantra meditation has you speak out a repeated or meaningless word or sound to anchor you in the present. In breathing meditation, you focus on your breath in order to stay in the moment. Mindfulness meditation

involves a conscious practice of nonjudgment and non-attachment while cultivating awareness of the present.
- It's best to have a routine as to when and where you meditate. Choose a time and place where you're relatively free from distractions. Most important is that your practice is consistent and that you approach it with a willingness to meet each moment with calm, kind awareness.
- Among the most common challenges in meditation are lack of consistency, expecting too much, impatience, low self-esteem and doubt, and an out-of-control, racing mind resulting from a highly stimulating day with a lot of stresses and unhealthy habits.
- It will take time to make meditation a habit, but you can help it along by attaching it to other daily habits you already have. Habit anchoring, a technique wherein you designate a thirty-second activity as a prompt for your meditation practice, helps you incorporate meditation more easily

in your daily life. You can also employ the habit loop formula, which consists of a cue, a reward, and a craving as elements of establishing a new routine.

CHAPTER 4. HOW TO OVERCOME AND DEFEAT EVERYDAY ERUPTIONS

- The practice of meditation and mindfulness does not need to be confined within a ten-minute session in a completely silent room—these techniques can be employed even during regular activities you do in your daily life.
- Whether you're writing a report, folding laundry, or tidying your desk, you can endeavor to engage in mindfulness. No matter who you are, how busy your life is or what challenges you are facing, you can always practice meditation and mindfulness. With effort and creativity, you can find ways to meditate at work, during errands or around the house.

- Practicing meditation does not mean that you can do away with life's humdrum routines after you've achieved heightened consciousness. Rather, meditating while you perform daily tasks will lead you to a deeper connection and genuine engagement with the present reality, along with its every routine chore and activity.
- Principles of mindfulness are especially useful when applied to reduce stress in the midst of life's hustle and bustle. Mindfulness-based stress reduction techniques help you break free of a hectic "doing" mode to a more tranquil yet purposeful "being" mode.
- A basic yet powerful technique in mindfulness practice is deep breathing. It involves breathing in through your nose and into your stomach, feeling your belly rise, and breathing out slowly through your mouth. This breathing exercise helps slow your heart rate, decrease

your blood pressure, and relaxes your body.
- Body scan, another stress-reduction technique, entails focusing your awareness on different parts of your body, one at a time. As you notice every sensation, tension, and discomfort you are experiencing, your body serves as an anchor to bring you to full awareness of the here-and-now.
- Visualization, a relaxation practice wherein you conjure a scene or image of something peaceful or calming, also helps relieve stress by steering your mind away from negativity and immersing it instead in a soothing mental picture.
- Stretching, a technique you can perform in itself or incorporate in your exercise routine, not only boosts your circulation and increases flexibility, but also helps calm the mind when done mindfully.
- With meditative habits ingrained in your everyday routine, you can meet every experience and sensation you

have with kind attention instead of heavy drudgery.

Chapter 5. A Path to Fulfilment and Satisfaction

- Done consistently, there is no area of life that meditation and mindfulness cannot improve. The more you immerse yourself in the practice of mindfulness, the more you'll experience the gloriousness of every moment you find yourself in, whether it's simply carrying out a common chore or facing an unprecedented challenge.
- Bad habits and addictions often emerge from a need to experience pleasure or avoid pain. Because of the benefits they offer you in the immediate moment, these activities get imprinted in your brain through repeated reinforcement. Over time, they become automatic, mindless crutches during your weak moments.
- Mindfulness is an antidote against a mindless succumbing to the pull of

bad habits. Cultivating mindfulness can help you break bad habits and manage your cravings by improving your self-control and bringing awareness and self-compassion to addiction cycles.

- Using mindfulness, you can disrupt bad habits at several points during their cycle. Right at the start, meet tempting triggers with calmness and equanimity. When you feel the urge to act, use mindfulness to notice the gap between impulse and action, and realize that engaging in the bad habit is not the only option. Even if you've already done the bad action, you can still employ mindfulness as you become aware that the rewards of such behavior are not as satisfying as you had anticipated after all.
- Mindfulness can improve self-control, help you manage cravings, break bad habits and bring awareness and compassion to addiction cycles.

- Mindfulness can help you better self-regulate through strong emotions such as fear and anger, by using mindful inquiry to gently tap into the deeper roots of our experience. Mindful inquiry has you resist from interpreting or analyzing anything, and instead leads you to approach your emotions with curiosity and an unconditional openness to simply observe and fully experience what is.
- Through mindfulness, we gain awareness of old patterns and tendencies we have acquired in our childhood or environment which do not work for us anymore, and we empower ourselves to choose actions and build habits that benefit us instead.
- Loving-kindness meditation can foster love and compassion for ourselves and others, which helps improve our emotional intelligence and interpersonal relationships.

CPSIA information can be obtained
at www.ICGtesting.com
Printed in the USA
LVHW021412250920
667085LV00006B/566